T0322496

I DON'T KNOW SH*T ABOUT F*CK

I DON'T KNOW SH*T ABOUT F*CK

RUTH LANGMORE

TITAN BOOKS

London, United Kingdom

CONTENTS

INTRODUCTION
YOU DON'T KNOW SHIT
ABOUT FUCK EITHER

You ever met somebody who's got a real high opinion of themselves, of their intellect or whatever, and then all of a sudden they just get blind-sided by the shit they don't know? They get stolen from, cheated on, or fuckin' killed? I mean, the men in my family were basically pit bulls that could speak English, only meaner. Those men didn't know anything, but they thought they knew *everything*—and that's a dangerous place to be. They thought they had everything all figured out, but they didn't have fuck-all figured.

That's why you gotta be smart about your stupid. Know what you know, know what you don't know, and know what you wanna know— and keep tabs on all of 'em. Hell, I think if some of the folks in my family had the wisdom deep down to know when they were being goddamn fools, they wouldn't have gotten themselves killed. Assuming that you're smarter than everyone is just about the dumbest move you can make, and you can quote me on that.

You see, that's what's at the heart of what I believe; that there's always something to learn, no matter who you are. I don't know shit about fuck and neither do you—no one does.

I mean, you ever seen someone with a fancy-ass college education try to calculate a tip for a waiter? It's like they've got worms for brains all of a sudden. Like adding 20 percent is suddenly a sum floating beyond the outer limits of their minds. The truth is they don't know shit about fuck, and if they just admitted it, if they'd just wave their waiter down and say "Give me a calculator, please" or "What do you think is fair, garçon?"

I bet that server would end up getting a decent tip and wouldn't have to go robbin' hotel rooms with their family every so often. You see my point? All it takes is a little willingness to stop pretending you know it all and everyone fuckin' wins.

To clarify, this isn't about trying to be ignorant. It's the opposite of that. It's really a way of learning, starting from admitting what you don't know. Approaching things from a place of not knowing shit is different than saying you don't want to learn shit, right? I think this helps people from the ground up. It helps someone who's hustling a few jobs get by a little easier if folks know how to tip right, and it helps those people giving out the tips not look like assholes. Most of all, looking at the world through the rose-colored glasses of not knowing shit about fuck helps people who are underestimated and underestimate themselves. I mean, look at me. I didn't go to college, but I've done pretty well for myself, all things considered. If I had pretended to know things, I wouldn't have gotten where I am.

Now, I used to complain about people reading self-help books, used to say self-help is the ultimate grift and that when I see people reading *The Secret* or whatever else, it would make me sick. See, the way I saw it, there ain't no way to fix yourself—you just are what you are. So buying any of those books, you're just out twenty bucks like a goddamn idiot. Now, I still think I was right about the grift, so I wanna be clear: This ain't no self-help book. This is just kinda how I see the world—and a couple of things that helped me step up and grow up. I'm just telling you to look at who you really are and what you actually know. And what you don't know.

The first thing I'll tell you about this way of growing yourself is that it fuckin' hurts. So, get ready for some pain, because fixin' the way you do things (which is basically tryin' to fix the way you are) hurts. Some people around you won't want you to do it. They'll see the change comin' and they'll put a goddamn boot on your neck to keep you down. I know that's what most of the people in my life did.

Don't get me wrong, I'm responsible for me and you're responsible for you, but changin', growin'. . . It'll mess your life up. Be willing to face that before you give up who you think you are.

Thankfully, I mostly thought I was a piece of shit before, so I didn't get real attached to who I thought I should be, I guess. Sure, I liked my people, my cousins, but taking care of them was a ton of responsibility for someone my age. I just pretended like I knew what I was doing raising them. I had to pretend that I knew everything about robbing hotel rooms and chopping boats and skimming money, even though I didn't. I knew the raw materials were there inside me, that I had some kinda smarts, I just wasn't sure of exactly what to do with 'em. But that was then . . . and I wouldn't have gotten to where I am if I didn't fake it just a little, but goddamn if I wasn't trying to ride a horse backward. And now? I've gotten past the idea that I know everything that I need to know, or that I can't learn new things. Now, I don't know shit about fuck.

The good thing about not knowing nothin' is that you've got everything to learn. The world is your fuckin' oyster. You think I knew anything about laundering money before I met Marty Byrde? No chance. Now, I'm not sayin' Marty knows shit, but he sure knows money. He knows money 'cause he's used to money. He's smart in that way, in a rich-person kinda way. Like money is the only thing he really knows. I wouldn't have been about to take my chances with Marty if I hadn't opened myself up to the possibility that I had been flyin' blind my whole life, up until that point. If I hadn't admitted to myself that deep down I don't know shit, I wouldn't be here now.

For me, I think not knowing shit makes every day new, kind of like you're a baby. It's kind of a spiritual state of mind or something. Like some people spend a fortune to go to Mexico or wherever to learn yoga or whatever, but I think they'd learn a hell of a lot more by livin' with me and my family in the middle of nowhere. I'll get 'em to clear their minds: There's nothin' to do out here, so there's nothin' to think about. If it's a "penny for your thoughts" kind of life, you'd have very little money coming your way out here.

The upshot of being from a "mind-clearing" type of place like where I'm from is that I've got the power of fuckin' perception on my side. What I mean by that is: People on the outside don't expect anything from me, and that allows me to move through the world without that kind of pressure. Nobody payin' attention to me. I've got no expectations for

myself or from other people, and after a while, folks start to take you for granted, and soon enough it's like you're just a leak in the roof. You're just one little drop at a time, no one really paying attention to you, and then, before you know it, the whole roof caves in. I'm the water in this situation, by the way: You might think I'm just a little bitty drop of rain, but believe me, I can fuck your shit up.

I know what people think of me and I know what I think of myself, and that's an important piece of this puzzle.

To all those fuckers doin' bad shit, I'm just a frizzy-haired girl who doesn't know a thing, and to all those Toyota-driving tourists, I'm just a piece of shit from the Ozarks. The best part about that? Well, it's like I get to sneak up on both types of people in the dark. Boo.

So if you've found yourself in a position where people don't expect much from you, don't worry about it. Take my example; sometimes it's important that people don't see you coming. And if you've managed to find yourself in a position where you have a task before you that you don't fully understand? Just remind yourself that you need to tell yourself you don't know shit about fuck and that's a good thing, that leaves you space to be a real detective about your situation, to ask questions, and really learn what the fuck you're doing. When you're scared or let down or just kind of feelin' like shit, ask yourself the question:

What's the most important thing that I, Ruth Langmore, know? Well, it's that I *want* to know fuckin' everything.

COMMIT TO THE CRIME

Being in a family like mine is almost like being in a family that owns a small business. My daddy taught me a trade, just like his daddy did and on and on. You get it. He had groomed me to steal since I was young enough to ask him to take me to the toy aisle for practice, so I really thought I knew my game by the time I decided to do something on my own for the first time.

It started because I liked this boy named Bodie, but he barely knew my name. I was fourteen and still going to school at that point, and even though he was nineteen he had flunked out enough that our classes stacked together pretty neatly. Now that I'm older it seems pretty clear that there was no way this nineteen-year-old boy was going to be interested in my fourteen-year-old self. Bodie was a lot of things, but he wasn't a fuckin' creep. Still, I hoped to turn his affections my way because I didn't know any better. One morning, I thought it would be cool if I offered him a cigarette at the laundry-mat behind the school, and you know what? It was. He took the cigarette and asked me if I wanted to cut class with some of his friends.

Now, let's be clear—it's not the cutting class that I'm choked up about; going to class is a waste of time if you live in the Ozarks. I wouldn't be surprised if you could find more of our "famous" spring water in the minds of our teachers than active, dynamic fuckin' thought. No, school wasn't for me, but skipping wasn't the part of my slide toward criminal behavior. That was already well underway.

It all started innocent enough: We were driving around looking for trouble, and when none presented itself, I was just hopin' that Bodie might turn to me in the back seat and lay one on me. No such luck though; those dumb shits all wanted to find some beer.

I said I knew where and how to get us some. I'd seen my daddy and uncles boost liquor a half dozen times when we didn't have much in the way of savings and the need for refreshments was high. Daddy would take us to the Savy 1 and direct me to sit in the driver's seat, should he need me to drive it in a pinch. That's right, I manned my first getaway car when I was eight. I never had to drive though—and who knows what would've happened if I did.

So we pull up to the Savy 1 and Bodie asks me to stay in the car while he and the boys go in to get the beer. They liked to think of it as a "transfer of ownership" rather than stealing, which is the first and last fuckin' rule in this chapter: Commit to the crime. You've gotta start with clear actions. If you're goin' to steal beer, then say to yourself "I'm goin' to steal beer." Don't be cute about it. Don't say you're transferring ownership of the beer. Confuses everyone. Being clever is about as stupid as anything.

Anyway, we pull up, park, and Bodie turns to me in the back seat and asks if I know what I'm doing. I get about the widest smile across my stupid face as I've ever had, looking at Bodie looking at me. It ain't until he leaves the car that I realize he's driving a fuckin' standard. Now, I've driven a standard. I can drive a standard now. But when I was fourteen? I still stalled out changing gears like I had hydraulics. In fact, that's what Russ would tease me about: "Girl, you look like you have fuckin' hydraulics in the car." So, what I should have done was chase Bodie into the store and pull him back to his car to explain I wasn't an expert driver yet, but as you can probably guess, I did no such thing. Instead I sank back into the seat of his car, hoping this thing would go okay.

I'd told Bodie that the cashier most likely was gonna be a man named Garret with a gnarled tree-root of a leg. I told him that he was lonely for folks to talk to him, which was something that I only imagined was true but didn't know for sure—I just assumed kind of, bein' that his leg was so twisted and his store was always so empty. I told him to go on in and strike up a conversation while the others gathered their supplies in back.

Last thing I told him was to yell "GO!" should it go sideways and they all need to bolt.

I heard him yell it about a half a second too late.

Even if the car hadn't stalled out, we didn't stand a chance. I'd been pressing my body against the back seat for some time, trying to squeeze myself out of existence. Hoping against hope the worst wouldn't happen, so when it did, my weight was tipped in the wrong direction.

I couldn't hop over the seats in time before the boys had dropped the beer, the cops had been called, and the whole thing was off.

If I flash back to when I first saw my daddy boost liquor, I can smell the car: like the last sip of beer and loose pennies in the console. I get lost in that metallic smell. Then I can hear it, the breath-heavy run to the car, the slam of the cases of beer into the trunk, Boyd and Russ and Daddy shouting, cheering each other on. The sound of the tires peeling out as we sped away from the Savy 1.

That's all I fuckin' knew about stealin' when I was a kid, was how it smelled, what it sounded like, who I was with, my family. I shouldn't have tried to do it without havin' learned properly how to go through it without my uncles or my daddy.

It's like when girls I knew asked their mamas for a recipe after watching them bake.

I just hadn't asked Cade Langmore how to strike out on my own yet.

This incident with Bodie happened a few months ahead of my reputation getting officially "Langmored," as they say. Meaning, I hadn't gotten caught participating in the family business of doing bad shit often enough for my tears to warrant suspicion. All I had to do was cry till snot came out of my nose and the police officers were off my case. I was too young for them to press any real charges against me anyway. Bodie got licked and had to spend the night in jail, and I lost track of him after that. It's pretty hard to lose track of people around here, especially if you're young—not to mention if you think you've found love, which I sure as shit thought I had.

After that, I didn't steal unless I asked Uncle Boyd or Uncle Russ or called up Cade in prison to lay it out for me real neat. Just 'cause I'd been following them around while they pulled shit off didn't mean

I had fully absorbed it. It was the first time I knew what I didn't know. I made it a point to plan out another beer run to the last fuckin' detail so I wouldn't get caught up like that again.

So, I made a list of the major things that tripped me up big: the stupid car, having the hots for Bodie, and thinking I knew everything. If I could get rid of those roadblocks, I might do all right. That was a real breakthrough moment for me—learning how to ask questions. So I kept asking questions, and asked and asked and asked. Got on my uncle Boyd's nerves real bad. The tricky part about absorbing other people's knowledge is this: You get smarter than them eventually; you grow out of your teachers. Happened with me and my uncles real quick, but more on that later (it's a goddamn tragedy they got so clinically fuckin' stupid).

When I was sure I'd lined it all up right, I had to beg some boys, other friends of Bodie, to come with me to do it again. My argument was that you can give a man fish or you can teach a man to fish. Or whatever the saying is. They agreed because of the beer.

The point is, I committed to the crime. I got my crew together, got really goddamn clear about what we wanted out of the night (an unlimited supply of beer), and then we set out to achieve our goal. Those boys thought I was stupid to try again and even more stupid when I took so much care around it, said it was like I was planning my own wedding, goddamn idiots. I wouldn't waste money on a fuckin' wedding.

We ended up getting our beer in the end, but those boys never thanked me, really. They ended up taking most of the beer for themselves, but I couldn't help but celebrate the fact that I'd successfully pulled off my first run. Cade was proud when I went to visit him next; he grinned real big and told me I was his girl. The thing is, Daddy just liked being a criminal—he liked what it meant, what it stood for.

Me? I just like to work, and to work, you gotta learn new things.

The only reason I was able to learn a thing from Marty Byrde was because I failed when I was younger. 'Cause I learned in short order that I didn't know the things I thought I did—that I didn't know everything I needed to get the job done right. And what I learned from Marty Byrde actually doesn't matter as much as the first lesson, where you give in to your own shortcomings and you commit to learning for the fuckin' betterment of yourself. That's the magic; that's the spell you cast that'll last you a lifetime. What you do with what you've learned, that's a minor detail: Whether it's stealing a boat or stealing a million, running a chop shop or running a casino . . . how you start learning is the most important part, and for me, that was the simple act of boosting liquor.

Stealing beer was a baby step; committing to the crime was the start of a new chapter in my life—one I still believe I'm in to this day.

Know what you're doing.
Do it.
Do it well.

CHAPTER
2

DEALING WITH YOUR CURSE

Have you ever heard of a self-fulfilling prophecy? You know, where someone says that they're absolutely not going to do something, and then before you know it they're doing exactly the thing that they said they weren't going to do? Like politicians. Or kings. Or like me.

My curse, my family's curse, is the curse of being smart as hell but trapped in a body full of bad impulses in a town that wants to swallow you whole. There ain't a stupid Langmore among us, but fuck if we don't get trapped and trap ourselves in all kinds of stupid situations.

In my family, when things aren't going well, we blame the "Langmore curse." We've been telling ourselves that there's a curse hanging over our heads for some time. I don't know if I believe it—depends on the day, depends on the moment. When I look at how many people in my family are dead, or the types of people we keep falling in with, I think it's got to be true. But when I look at Wyatt, and all of the possibility that having a mind like that can bring, I think there's hope and that you make your own fate.

At this point, the Langmore curse is practically a part of Ozark mythology. People see us coming and their noses turn up: They know we bring the unlucky stink with us. It's not that we're stupid, it's that we have stupid luck, so normal things are harder. Have you ever seen a family with no women? Can you imagine my luck to get stuck with a herd of men? Most of my friends (not that there are many) get stuck with their moms and with their moms' boyfriends. It's the dads that leave. But me? No, I had to deal with five men. Alone. Don't believe me about the curse? Just look at this family:

First you got Cade Langmore, the patriarch of the family and unfortunately my father. He does his time in prison but then he gets himself killed almost as soon as he gets out. Thing about Daddy is that he was smarter than most people—he could figure out just about any part on any car or boat stolen or found, and he had a bloodhound sense about whether or not people had money to part with. He just couldn't figure out when to stop; if he stole from someone, he wanted to make sure he squeezed out every drop. He'd take too many risks for his pride in making a big score. As far as I see it, pride was his curse. He was proud of being the baddest fuckin' man who ever walked out of jail with all ten fingers and toes. I waited for my daddy to come back for ten years, and when he got here he wasn't any good to me. It was like something had boiled over in him and he couldn't see me. Like I was still a kid, riding bitch in the back seat of his car.

Next up is Boyd: I don't have a goddamn lot to say about Boyd except he was trouble for no reason. That man had a lip on him like he knew everything. I'm not saying I didn't have goddamn love in my heart for him, because I did. It's just that he didn't know when to shut up. He was basically the mouthy version of my daddy. If Daddy always took things too far in action, Boyd always took it too far in word. I miss him, I do, and I wish he were still alive, but it was almost as if he liked the Langmore curse sometimes.

I didn't have no problem with Russ until I had a problem with Russ, you know what I mean? I knew he had a hard time because some people thought he was gay and he just couldn't live with that. And that's so fuckin' sad I can barely think about it. Talk about a curse: being born into a family like ours where bein' a tough guy is a currency as good as the dollar—and underneath all that, you're hidin' a big fuckin' secret? Fuck, that'd be too much for me. Hard part of it was that Russ, without even trying, was tougher than fuckin' nails. Could take a hit with the best of them and then give it right back. He didn't need to go around acting like a big man. He was a big man. Anyway, I didn't have a single problem with that man until he started talking to the goddamn FBI. Don't fuckin' snitch. That's a big part of my philosophy too. Especially don't snitch on your family. Especially when they're Langmores.

I guess you could say that Russ's curse was that he had so much to hide his whole life, that's what ended up killing him. He could have figured out a way to come to me with his trouble, but instead he hid.

My cousin Wyatt's curse is that he's too fuckin' smart and sensitive to be part of this family. I think it must be traumatizing to be smart in a place that's so dumb. A place full of people who are so rough. I've always been allergic to seein' him sad, so I tried to get him out of here. I guess I messed that up.

Oh, I care about my cousin Three too; I can hear you wondering why I don't give a shit about Three, but I love him. It's just that Wyatt is smart. He's the smartest Langmore in the world, even if there are some fuckin' Nobel prize–winning Langmores somewhere out there I don't know about. Wyatt's different, and he's different in a place that doesn't want you to be different. This is a place that wants to reabsorb you, let you know that you are of the Ozarks, that you were born here and you'll die here, and that even if you leave here, you've got that lake water inside you. Best to accept you'll fall victim to some gruesome death of poverty or crime, and in that life cycle you'll become a tree, or, in my family's case, mulch.

Maybe Wyatt's curse is that I want him to be better than the rest of us. That's a lot of fuckin' pressure. Maybe his curse is me. Maybe I am the Langmore curse. I push people too far.

Take, for instance, when I wrangled Russ and Boyd to steal from the Byrde family that first week they were down here. Now, we were all in over our heads when we did that, I'll admit, but once Marty got clear with us about what would happen to us if we spent that cash on big-ticket items, I squirreled that shit away. But Russ and Boyd? Those two thought that just because we found some money, we were suddenly lucky. Like our curse had just vanished. Idiots. It's like those two would just up and forget who we were, like they had amnesia. At the end of the day though, that shit was my fault. I was pushing my uncles into a crime they weren't capable of executing.

I had my reasons for wanting that money, obviously. We were hard up as fuck, you know? Dirt poor. I know how to be poor, but I was sick of it. Most people don't know how to be poor; shit, most people don't even know that it's a *skill*. When you've got two jobs and you gotta figure out the best way to do a single load of laundry for a family of six with one load's worth of quarters, you get good at a different kind of math. I did that math for my family: the money and the jobs and the meals and the laundry. All that shit fell to me when my daddy went to jail—and even before.

I was so sick of hustling at being poor when I saw Marty Byrde's money, when I sniffed it out in his hotel room. I could feel something growling inside me, something burning and hungry because I was so excited. I'd found the thing that was gonna save us from petty crime and shitty jobs for a long fuckin' time, if not forever.

Sometimes it comes in handy to have a family that's willing to do the stupid things I ask them to. Like going and stealing a suitcase full of money from a stranger in a cheap hotel. We knew that money probably had connections that could get our fingernails peeled off slow, but my uncles said FUCK YES we'll take the risk.

Now, there are two ways of thinking about the events that followed after stealing that money and me getting linked up with the Byrde family. The first thought I have is that diving into that particular heist enabled me to level up and learn how to launder money. I didn't even know I needed to worry about clean money versus dirty money; wasn't even on my radar. So if I hadn't had a family that was crazy enough or cursed enough to jump into the deep end with me and rob Marty Byrde blind, I might not know what I know now; hell, I might be in jail or dead or close to it.

The second (and more glass-half-empty) way of thinking about it is that I didn't know what I was getting into and I got fucked. I stole money, and not only did Marty mostly take it back, but he roped me into his family and I ended up betraying my people—which is almost as bad as snitching, if you ask me.

I'm going to take this opportunity to be a silver-lining kind of person and say that because I didn't know what the fuck I was getting into and neither did my family, and being that we were inclined to steal everything that wasn't bolted down in those hotel rooms anyway, I'm glad we did what we did. I learned what I didn't know because my uncles were brave enough or stupid enough or crazy enough (or some combination of all three) to follow me into battle.

Having what others might refer to as a cursed family helped me get ahead in the end, 'cause there was nothing that was ever normal about us. Never had a packed lunch or a kiss on the top of my head (which is what I imagine the Byrdes do to their little towheaded girl, Charlotte Byrde, before she prances off to school). I didn't have the burden of expectations hanging over my head. No one expected me to go to a nice school or meet a nice boy or any of that shit, and I didn't expect shit from life either. Not having anything, not growing up with anything except the eruptions of violence, discord, and the occasional celebration of riches cribbed from this or that establishment, made me formidable as a businesswoman, helped me take risks. If you've got nothing to lose or even if you're cursed, why the fuck not?

CHAPTER

3

KEEP THEM GUESSING

There are few advantages to bein' small in stature, but I will list them here: Airplane rides are generally more comfortable (I've heard), most hand-me-downs fit you, and lastly, nobody expects you to fight back when it comes down to it.

I know I'm a Langmore, but that didn't mean that folks expected me to have a mean right hook—I barely weigh a hundred pounds. If people fucked with me, they knew they were really fuckin' with Cade and Russ and Boyd, but after Cade went to jail, I was left without a real protector. Sure, Daddy wasn't what you'd call chivalrous, but you can't accuse him of bein' unsentimental about his family connections. I mean, the idea that I had fallen in with a family like the Byrdes—that is, a family that is not ours—made my daddy homicidal. That said, he still wasn't around to teach me to fight when I needed to learn.

Thing is, I was kind of a funny-looking kid. I was real lanky with this frizzy blond, almost white hair. It's not an ideal collection of features to this day, if you ask me, but back then, when I was growin' up—fuck if I didn't hear every joke about God rainin' ugly on me that there ever was.

Back in middle school was when I got the worst of it, especially from boys—especially from Keith Robisheaux. Keith was my first real nemesis; he'd give me lip about bein' ugly and I'd give it back and try not to cry. I was upset that it was a boy makin' fun, bein' that I grew up with nothin' but boys and thought I knew how to handle them okay. He was the kind of guy who would thud around lookin' for somebody to pick on so he could look a little bit taller. Literally, he'd usually pick the smallest person he could find to pick on. He had the bulk of a football player too, so he was no joke to scrap with. I once saw him dismantle a kid's jaw with one blow to the face. He loved fighting was the thing.

One day, I was minding my own business, walkin' down the hall, when I felt the wind knocked out of me all of a sudden. Before I could realize what'd happened, I was flat on my stomach. This motherfucker Keith Robisheaux had slammed his bag full of textbooks square into the middle of my back—threw me right to the ground. When he walked by, he dropped the bag on top of me, then squatted down next to me while I was gasping for air and whispered, "Looks like you're takin' a nap, Langmore."

Keith slammed his books and fists down on my back for what seemed like hours. I know it was probably only three minutes, but it was enough to turn me black and blue. There's something humiliating about bruising, like your skin can't stand up to punishment. And the pain after, it's like bein' haunted by your own flesh. Keith had a remarkable talent for not getting caught, if you asked me; either that or the teachers were too scared to discipline him.

When I first told my uncles about what Keith Robisheaux had done to me, they wanted to go kick his ass. They wanted to kick his ass and find his whole family and kick their asses. The sight of me with welts and bruises on my back made them feral. But I insisted: I wanted to learn how to fight. I knew that's what my daddy would want too, and if he weren't locked up that's what he would have told me: Learn to fight, stick up for yourself.

So, Russ tried to teach me whatever fuckin' bullfighting he knew, the swings and blows that make you look cool, but Boyd was more help. See, Boyd was a string bean like me; he looked like a scarecrow till his dyin' fuckin' day. After an exhausting afternoon of gasping and trying to get a hit in with Russ, Boyd pulled me to the side and gave me a beer. I thought I was finally getting relief from fightin' but Boyd pulled the beer out of my hand, broke the goddamn bottle, and thrust the sharp end in my face.

Then he replaced my beer.

He told me that the biggest asset I had when I was fighting was being a girl. Told me to keep my teeth sharp and my nails long, 'cause there was no goddamn way I was going to outswing a hulk like Keith Robisheaux. No matter how many times Russ taught me his moves, I'd never have the physics behind his brute force, so I had to play by my own rules.

The rules were:

Go for his nuts.

Go for his eyes.

Use your nails.

Use your teeth.

Kick.

Bite.

Scratch.

Fight like a bitch, get that fucker off you, and then run. There is no honor in fighting fair—only in winning.

Another rule: Find someone smaller than you to kick the shit out of. Make a point without talking. See, Boyd had been locked up more than a few times at that point, and every time he went to the big house somebody would take his ass to the mat. Thing was, Boyd believed that you could scare people with your violence even if you were just burning ants on the sidewalk. So he had no reservations about bringing hurt to someone smaller. He told me it was part of the goddamn food chain. To be clear, I don't believe that kind of shit anymore. Not with the way I felt after.

Next time I walked into school wasn't for a couple of weeks, being that I had to heal from the incident with Keith and my uncles were pretty relaxed about my school attendance. The halls looked different to me, electric with tension. Nobody looked at me any different than they had before, but I knew I was different, and that made the place shift around me, made everyone else different to me.

Josh Fardin.

Josh Fardin had the misfortune of being even smaller than me. Probably too small for someone like Keith to even bother with picking on. Doesn't mean that he didn't get picked on by other kids—he just wasn't particularly interesting to Keith. Josh was the kind of kid who would go to classes at the local community college for fun but would flunk out of regular school because he thought it was beneath him. This little fucker thought everything was beneath him even though he barely cleared five feet above ground. Plus his last name was Fardin; there wasn't much time in the day that this kid wasn't getting made fun of. It didn't help that his mother was the president of the PTA and was constantly advocating for an honors program at our school. Dumb bitch didn't realize you'd need a teacher with two brain cells to rub together to teach a goddamn honors course.

Josh was a rare individual, and as I've said, being a rare individual in the Ozarks isn't a good thing. He was always explaining things to people so they'd feel like the dumbest fuckin' people on the planet, especially me. Like he'd pick up on something not being quite right and he'd throw around the word *Orwellian* like we're all supposed to know what *Orwellian* means, even though none of us except future Wyatt had read Orwell. It was a classic Josh move to just see him chomping down on someone in the middle of the hallway for not knowing what the word *Orwellian* meant. He was used to getting threatened, but most people didn't even see the point giving the backside of your hand to a boy like that—he'd most likely talk your ear off while you were beating the shit out of him.

So Josh was at his locker with his arms full of books, scowling into the darkness, scratching his head. I remember he had to get on his tip-toes to see all the way to the back of his locker; he looked more like a toddler than a middle school kid from behind. Just as his head tipped between the door and the frame, I felt myself growl:

Don't call me no fuckin' whore. I'll kill your whole motherfuckin' family.

To be clear, Josh didn't call me a whore. He didn't say a word to me that day. Josh had, however, called me a harlot a number of times, being that he thought I wouldn't know what that meant. That had been weeks ago though. When I saw Josh that day, I still had the ghost of those bruises on my back from Keith and the drunken fight lessons with Russ and Boyd. I still had a daddy in jail. I still had frizzy hair and weak muscles. I still had fear and hunger every fuckin' day. And looking at

Josh that morning, I felt that all boil over inside of me. I felt like I was gonna melt down if I didn't hurt someone.

I slammed his head into the locker three times fast.

After he dropped to the ground, he propped himself up as best he could and tried to sort of form a claw with his small white hand. I noticed his fingernails were long, which for the record is just about the most foul thing a boy can do, grow his nails. He flailed at my face while I put a hand in the middle of his chest and held him down. He said:

You lie. You lie. You lie.

A circle of kids formed around us pretty fast. Nobody could believe that someone was bothering with Josh Fardin. Nobody could believe that *I* was bothering with Josh Fardin. I made sure to find Keith in the circle and make eye contact with him before I swung my fist down on Josh's face as hard as I could, which wasn't very hard. Ended up kind of bouncing off his jaw, so I reached down and scratched across his eye. At least I tried. I felt the meat of someone's arm pulling me off of Josh before I could do too much damage.

Things went pretty much like I thought they would after that. I ended up suspended, he ended up suspended. I ended up more suspended because I didn't have what you would call an appropriate advocate in Russ or Boyd, and Josh had his mother there with her crucifix and her library card and her certainty that I was the Antichrist. I didn't see the harm in missing a few days of school, but Mrs. Fardin thought that the school would be missing out on Josh. I personally think that they were glad to get rid of him for a few days; I doubt anyone on staff knew what *Orwellian* meant either.

By the time I got back to school, I had put some respectful distance between Keith Robisheaux and me. He would even end up inviting me to a party at an empty trailer park later that year—that's how much space I created with that fight. I really think it was because I showed people that I didn't give a shit. That I'd fight anyone. I was feral. Of course, Josh didn't see it that way. I feel a little lump in my stomach about it sometimes. Sure, he spent most of the time I knew him finding fancy ways to call me an idiot and a whore, but that don't mean I feel great about using him to intimidate Keith. Needed to be done, but I didn't enjoy it. In fact, after I made a show of how weak Josh Fardin was, I started to think about him more and more.

You ever dream of someone you hurt?

I dream about Russ and Boyd. Cade. Wyatt. But Josh was the first one I had dreams about after hurting him. That's what you gotta deal with after a fight. After blood gets spilled. Those thoughts around it: Josh at home with his mom and his books. Josh without any physical strength. Josh without friends. Josh's red face if he ever had to tell his daddy (if he ever knew him) that he got whupped by a goddamn girl. Josh and his mother ended up moving to Fayetteville, I think.

The important thing isn't that I learned how to fight—it's that I learned how *I* fight. Some people are good at swinging fists and fightin' fair, some people aren't good for nothing except taking a beating or running as fast as they can, some people meet a problem head-on, and some people hide. How do I fight? I scratch my problem in the eyes, I distract my problem and then kick it in the knees, I pull my problem's hair. I'm not saying it always works, but part of knowing how you fight is knowing how you *win*. I know I'm not going to win a fight by training like Rocky. That's never going to happen. Same way I'm not going to earn buckets of money by inventing an app or splitting atoms or whatever. But that doesn't mean I'm not smart or tough. I just always bust in the back door of an establishment. That's my way.

The truth is I wouldn't know what I know about myself if I hadn't had a hard go of it. If Keith hadn't dropped bags full of books on me till I had bruises. But shit, if I hadn't had uncles with bad tempers, maybe I wouldn't have a temper either.

If I hadn't had a father with a temper, maybe I'd still have a father.

You never know is my point.

But I fight how I fight and I don't fool myself about how I do it. I don't have to trip over my fuckin' honor every time I want to get ahead in the world, and that's been the one thing that's saved me again and again. Ruth Langmore doesn't fight with honor. Ruth Langmore doesn't take sides.

CHAPTER

4

DON'T TELL PEOPLE SHIT

You want to know how I can tell someone is really full of shit? They can't stop talking. It's what a high-dollar therapist would call a fuckin' compulsion. You know the type—they just can't shut up about how good they are at doin' any old thing. No one likes to work with this person, no one likes to live with this person, and there are very few people who like to be friends with this person. There are always a few idiots who can get bowled over by the smoke and mirrors of someone who talks a lot of shit, but that isn't me. I don't believe that someone can do something until I actually see them do it.

Talking about what you do is bad for two reasons: First, it just wastes a lot of time. What if it were someone coming to collect the trash, and instead of just dumpin' the cans in their truck and movin' right along, the drivers got out of their truck and woke you up at the ass crack of dawn to say, "Hey, I don't know if you know this, but I never spill." No, that shit would be unacceptable. The public in general wouldn't stand for it. Same goes for any kinda crime you're gonna commit. It's a job. Don't talk, just do. Second reason it's bad is that it's goddamn dangerous.

Don't tell someone how good you are at fightin', just sock 'em in the face when it's appropriate. Don't tell someone you're gonna kill 'em. Just make them dead if you need them to be.

Of course, what I'm edging around here is the most serious offense when it comes to not telling people shit. It's hard to get into, but get into it I must. Don't fuckin' snitch. Don't talk to the motherfuckin' FBI.

I know, I know, Russ didn't know he was talkin' to the FBI at first, he was just fallin' in love with his beau and some truly unhelpful shit just fell out of his stupid mouth. I know he didn't put us in that position on purpose. But that's why you don't talk. Why you don't tell people shit. Truth is, you never know who you're talkin' to, even when you're talking to your own family. Russ proved that point when he put on a wire.

If Russ hadn't gotten it into his head to talk to that FBI agent about Marty Byrde's money, I sincerely believe that he and Boyd would still be alive today. Wyatt and Three would still have a daddy, and even if that daddy is a fuckup like Russ, he still would have been better than nothing.

Who knows what would have happened if Boyd and Russ were still alive; maybe I wouldn't have gotten in so deep with the Byrdes. Maybe Wyatt could have gone to state school just like we've talked about forever. But no, Russ had to strap on a fuckin' wire. Made himself dangerous to me. Truth is, the FBI is what makes criminals so dangerous. I've never seen Russ act more like a scared animal than when he was wired, and once a person is scared, they're dangerous. Hell, it was only after the FBI wired him up that Russ decided to strike out on his own to kill Marty. Once they've got you, you might as well go lookin' for a comfortable way to die; rather that than running your mouth and ruining people's lives.

The key is to shut the fuck up and only engage in the bare minimum of polite (with standard exceptions) conversation that it takes to get something done. If someone seems like they're a little too interested in one particular topic and it don't make no sense, then it don't make no sense and don't tell them shit, even the bare minimum. People who are just trying to forge ahead and get their shit done don't do extra talking. If anyone ever says to you "Just tell me" or "I won't tell," all the more reason not to tell that person anything. When someone says that they won't tell, then that means they can't wait to tell. It means they're so hungry for information that they'd cut you open for it. That counts for insider information at work as much as it counts for neighborhood gossip.

Another good rule of thumb for talking to people is this: Don't tell people something that you wouldn't want everybody knowing. If it can't be everybody's business, it can't be anybody's business. Look at other people as though they are simply a delivery service for your per-

bound to by a desperate necessity, by the fear of life and death. And once you step out of that shadow? There isn't anyone you can trust. No friends, no family, no great loves of your life. Trusting people with your secrets can make you feel kind of light, like you're being unburdened from the weight of the world, but it can also get you fuckin' killed. Don't let that temptation take over. I know that there have been times that I've found comfort in the strangest places, and I've wanted to confide.

There've also been times when I've wanted to snitch so fuckin' bad that it made my teeth ache. Not to the cops, mind you, but to some imagined power that could strike down my enemies. When I was hurt, when I am hurt, I can't tell you how many imagined wars I've set into action by passing around the right information.

Like when Wendy went away with Ben. I knew she wasn't up to any good, couldn't have been, her brother was so out of control. I knew if I set her in the sights of law enforcement as they drove away, she'd have gotten caught. Ben would have too, but he wouldn't be dead.

But I didn't do it. Because it never ends well, and destroying my rep as someone who can keep a secret wouldn't be worth it. We can talk about revenge later, but for now, don't tell people shit. No exceptions.

CHAPTER

5

FIGURE OUT WHO TO KILL

I remember the first time Daddy killed someone. Or the first time I knew that he was a killer. He was all hopped up, like he was high, but he wasn't. It was the kill that made him high. Made him talk a mile a minute. I know a little about PTSD now that I've been hanging around people like Wendy and Marty. I know that an animal part of the mind takes over when a person is in a clusterfuck situation like a shooting or a robbery. Even a car accident. I know that all those chemicals and hormones can make a person feel like Superman. And I know that that's what Cade Langmore felt like that night, the night that he became a killer to me: He felt like a superman, running on the adrenaline of being an animal that had killed another animal. Pure and simple.

To say it scared me is an understatement. I didn't ever want to be that, but I did make friends with the fact that I might have to kill too someday. Cade even talked me through it, the way a mother would give her daughter a talk about the birds and the bees. Daddy talked me through my first time too.

Except he thought he was talkin' me through killing Marty Byrde.

Now, I didn't kill Russ and Boyd out of any sense of loyalty to Marty. Let's get that out in the open right away. I killed Russ and Boyd 'cause they were going to ruin Wyatt and Three's whole lives. If my uncles had managed to get Marty's money, which was a long shot in the first place, then they would have had to manage making it to Canada without getting so much as a speeding ticket. Even if they had gotten the money, hauled their asses up to Canada completely undetected by the FBI, and set up shop there with the boys, they wouldn't have known how to create new identities or get their cash clean. They all would have been FUCKED.

Russ was just fucked. He wasn't going to get out of the situation he was in without some pain. He should have just done the right thing, taken his lumps, and gone to jail. It's like I said before—don't tell people shit.

It was his own fault he was in trouble, but he decided I needed to pay the bill.

I was surprised that Daddy wasn't more understanding of my situation, even for Daddy. Those men, my uncles, were trying to ruin my life. Not only were they going to kidnap my employer and steal my only source of income, but they were going to leave me stranded by myself in the Ozarks. One of the only things that makes life bearable here is the people you got around you; if you don't have that, you don't have shit. They forced my hand by pursuing the murder of Marty Byrde, mainly because they were bein' such dumb fucks about it. I found myself at a crossroads between my uncles and my boss. Normally it'd be family all the way, but sometimes you have to stop, think, and figure out who you're gonna kill. In my case, it was my boss or my uncles.

First step to figuring it out is accepting that you're going to have to kill someone; the second step is accepting that you may be a killer. Or maybe it's the other way around. Chicken-or-the-egg kind of situation.

How do you know if you're a killer? Look in the goddamn mirror. If you see a human staring back at you, then congratulations, you're a killer. Everyone is a killer. My daddy, my uncles, Marty (sure, he kills passively, but he kills), everyone I know has a body count. There are just those of us who get our hands a little bit dirtier than others. Some sick fucks like it, but I don't. Some chickenshits think they've got their hands clean, but they don't. Nobody does. Nobody's free of this shit.

Once you've accepted your nature as a predator, you're already halfway there, but just because people are natural killers, remember: Firing a gun isn't for everybody.

People like my daddy? People who get high off of killing? Those people are rare. Daddy didn't have to decide who to kill, 'cause everyone was on the chopping block. Yeah, even me. Especially after he got out of prison. See, he thought I had chickened out of killing Marty, and that just wasn't true. An important footnote or whatever the fuck you call it is that I had earnestly decided to kill Marty Byrde and take his money. I did this because I had pressure from my family to do it. I made the right decision, if you ask me. Marty might have even thanked me in the end if I had done it. It was Russ that stopped me. Russ who made my decision complicated when he broke down my electric rigging at the dock. Can you imagine thinking someone was as good as dead and then watching them walk away from you on their two legs? Shit.

Point being: Sometimes the choice is made for you.

Sometimes fate intervenes on your behalf.

The important thing is that I had decided who to kill. I tried to stick by my family's side, do what they wanted, kill the man with the money, but they weren't gonna let me have it, and there was no goddamn scenario where everyone in that situation could remain among the living.

People who snitch are living on borrowed time anyway.

I'm sad that Russ had to drag Boyd into it though. I'm sad either of them got dragged into it, to be honest. Life would have been a lot easier without all that death hanging around.

That's the ultimate question you gotta ask yourself when deciding who you're gonna kill: Whose ghosts are you comfortable with? Who can you carry with you comfortably for the remainder of your days? Because that's what you're going to have to do—carry those invisible bodies until you return to dust yourself.

I think the scariest thing about realizing that Daddy was a killer was knowing that we were made out of the same material, the same guts, had the same word running through our minds: *survive*. But I have to believe that Cade's wires got crossed somewhere, and that's the place where we start splintering off in different directions as father and daughter. I kill for necessity; he killed for rage at the world—I hope, I think he just wanted to eat the whole world up at the end and then there was no way he could survive. It's because he didn't take his time deciding who to kill.

Let it be known: This decision will ruin your life no matter what you choose, but choose you must.

Choose wisely.

CHAPTER

6

THREATEN YOUR EMPLOYER

Every once in a while you gotta swing a dick. There's no two ways about it. You have to make your presence known to people and make demands so that people know your worth. More importantly, you gotta show people how far you'll fuckin' go to get what you want. If you think about it, society is pretty much built on threats. Threat of war, of hunger, of poverty—threat of all kinds of danger, really. There are larger threats but there are petty ones too: fear that your husband or wife will leave you, the threat of losing your job, that your kids will fuckin' hate you—you get it. Life is basically threatening all the fuckin' time, and on occasion you gotta do the same thing.

So, how do you get any leverage when you're coming from what I would call an "underdog"-type position? You gotta threaten the person who holds power over you. Or thinks they hold power over you. When someone like a Marty Byrde walks in your door and he's got cash in hand and a cartel at his back, you know the only thing you can take from a person like that is his life, or the life of his family. Now, I'd never threaten children—that's a shit-heel move and I don't think it's worth being alive if you're going to be the kind of person who scares kids to get ahead. But real, grown-ass people? Fuck yeah I'll threaten them.

Now, sometimes it's just for show, but you have to be willing to follow up as a last resort. Like with Marty when I stole his money. I had a real good grip on his attention when I was threatening him in front of my cousins. I know for a fact that men get scared when they see a woman with a pack of men behind her. That was before Russ and

Boyd blew it, but I'm sure for that moment when I was talking to Marty about his certain death at the hands of the Langmores, right then and there, that's where the seed of respect was planted. He knew that I was a person who was willing to walk the walk, not just talk the talk.

Later on, when I decided to go into the Blue Cat and claim my job, it helped that Marty already knew I was a threat. Hell, I knew it was my fault that I got fired from that shitty hotel for stealing, and I know it's my fault that I got a rap sheet. What isn't my fault is that I was born into the kind of family that didn't give me no other options but to be a fuckup. But you wouldn't know that I knew all that when I gave it to Marty about how he fucked up my life by getting me fired. I made it clear that without my cooperation, his life in the Ozarks was going to be some kind of painful. I mean, I guess it ended up being pretty fuckin' painful anyway. For both of us, but at least I made a little coin.

Part of what was important about the way that I threatened Marty was that I didn't at any point make it seem like it was ever going to be all the way safe with me around. My silence had to be bought not just in that moment, but for all of time. Or he'd have to kill me, which I knew he just didn't have the stomach for at that point. After that, I'm not gonna say that it was smooth sailing, but having the balls to threaten someone does open doors. In a business like this, you have to be able to throw your weight around, even if you're a featherweight like me. While I'm not happy about what it's all done to my family, I wouldn't even consider taking back all the lessons I've learned.

It's kind of like an advanced version of fighting. Fighting by knowing you can, by knowing you have the guts to follow through, that you have the guts to lose, that you're pretty sure you know what it'd be like to die. Folks don't mess with you as easy when you've got that look in your eye.

Threatening your employer might seem like a stupid move, but that's the point. It *is* a stupid move. It's the kind of stupid move that makes people think you're dangerous because they have no fuckin' idea just how far you'll go or how stupid you're willing to get. It gives you the upper hand.

Take, for instance, when Frank Jr. was mouthin' off to me 'cause I kicked him out of the *Missouri Belle*'s first high-stakes card game. Now, that fuck-nut is the son of the head of the KC mob, so by all accounts I should be terrified of him. And that's what he assumed time after time. He was real surprised when I took him out, and more than a little pissed. The stupid/smart thing I did that night was show up as exactly who I am. I didn't start being some polite young woman 'cause a daddy's boy was upset. No, I told him exactly who I thought he was and told him with a smile on my face that he could come get him some. Then I kicked him in the nuts and threw him off the boat.

Doing that was stupid. It made Frank Sr. wanna take my life, but instead, it made Marty have to step forward and say that I'm untouchable. You wouldn't think that making a stupid move like humiliating your boss's partner's son would be a good idea, but goddamn if it didn't end up playing my way. Well, for the moment. But I knew in the back of my mind I might have to reckon with that not going my way. Nobody is really ever untouchable is what I'm learning.

Daddy taught me to be beholden to no one. Except him. Other than that, no one had jurisdiction over Ruth Langmore. Not Marty, not my uncles, not my friends, and not even the KC mob. It's not just about the words coming out of your mouth, it's about ignoring other people's power over you. Threatening someone who holds power over you (like a boss of any kind) means you're pretending, just for the moment, that you don't give a shit about their power.

Folks hate it when you won't acknowledge their power.

Now, I bet you're wondering what to do if you run across someone who can't be intimidated with threats. It's a simple answer but I'll spell it out: Follow through. I said it before and I'll say it again: You have to be willing to follow up a threat with action. For example, if Marty hadn't been smart enough to give me a job at the Blue Cat and get this whole crazy mess going, I would have gone on a campaign of terror about his stash of money. There's no one who wouldn't have known about it: the tourists, the Snells—hell, I would have gotten in touch with the fuckin' cartel in Mexico if I could have dialed that number direct.

Threats can't be empty. People can feel it when they are, because *you* can feel it when they are: It's a shaking kind of feeling in your bones.

Now, don't walk into a situation like a pissed-off girl giving her boyfriend an ultimatum about some stupid engagement ring. You know how many people I know do shit like that? They say they're gonna leave someone if they don't do this or buy them that or stop drinkin' or come meet the family, but then when it comes down to it? They roll the fuck over. A good exercise before you go in to threaten someone is this: Picture what your life would be like if this shit doesn't happen the way you want it to. Get specific. That's what I did. I made a detailed list of the things I'd do if I hadn't gotten the job at the Blue Cat, and Marty could see it on my face. I was gonna follow through.

Now, that's not the same as thinking things through, like thinking about the consequences or whatever—it's just thinking about the plan laid out in front of you and following it to the end. Those are two totally different things, plans and consequences, and two totally different ways of thinking.

People used to think that I was dangerous because I didn't think before I acted. I remember any number of adults in my life outside of the Langmore family confronting me about thinking before I act. *Why don't you think before you act, Ruth Langmore? You wanna ruin your life like your daddy?* At the end of the day, the reason that people should actually be terrified of me is because I do think. I push my mind to really think about what I'm going to do in a situation if I don't get what I want. Sure, I get a hot temper and end up smashing shit as good as the next person, but when I really put my mind to it, when I really want something, I've got it all planned out.

Figure out what you'd be willing to smash shit up for, then make it known. What is a threat if not making your desires known?

CHAPTER

7

SPY ON EVERYBODY

You know how when parents are raising their babies, they work so hard to get them to say "Mama" and "Daddy" or whatever? But then by the time those kids are toddlers, they're just repeating every goddamn thing their parents say. The parents realize pretty damn quick that they can't say "fuck," "shit," "damn," "cunt," or any manner of curse words unless they want them to repeat every goddamn one of 'em. And even though everybody knows this about kids, they still go ahead and talk shit around kids because they think maybe they ain't listening, like maybe that's the one kid in the whole universe who's actually minding their business. Well, anyway, I try to be that kid, the quiet kid. It's important to lay low and look like you're doing something else when you're not actively defending yourself or attacking someone else.

When I was working at the hotel and those Byrdes flew in, I wasn't just replacing towels because I was a model fuckin' employee; I was replacing towels because I knew I'd get to their room, and I knew there'd be a story once they got there.

Now, I have to say, because I don't want no one thinking I'm someone who doesn't live by a code: Spying is the *opposite* of snitching. While I don't believe in telling secrets, I don't think it's a problem if I happen to discover someone else's. I'd sooner cut off one of my own toes than tell the FBI what's going on with someone on my side of the net. Hell, even though I killed Russ and Boyd, I still didn't tell Marty all about why until my daddy blew that up. I wasn't even gonna snitch on Russ for snitching, that's how against snitching I am.

However, getting information on persons of interest and whatnot? That's a different fuckin' story. You've got to keep your eyes open wide for important information wherever you may go. You'll notice all kinds of things if you assume that there's always something to notice, even in places you've been a million times.

As I see it, there are about three types of spying:

First type and my personal favorite, which I have been the master of for some time now, is the "Oh, I'm not doing nothing over here" type of spying. Now, I think it's pretty clear what I mean by that, but I'll clarify for the sake of being fuckin' crystal. So, let's say you got a job, like washing dishes at the Blue Cat or a similar-type establishment to the Blue Cat, even a Denny's or a Waffle House. So let's say that you're just washing those dishes like you're in the Olympics of dishwashing, like you've been training to do it your whole life, really making a big deal about minding your own business. That step is key: looking like you're minding your own business.

I'd say that this type of spying, the playing-dumb type of spying, falls most directly in line with not knowing shit about fuck. It's like you're performing not knowing shit about fuck, and it's a beautiful thing, because people don't expect you to be watching them when they think you don't know anything.

Let's say that you see a nice family come into your place of work and you recognize them. You not only recognize them, but goddamn if you don't just happen to know where they live, 'cause last time you seen them come in you might have gotten a wild hair to figure out exactly where they live. So you're washing those dirty dishes and you happen to think, *Well, my family should know that this nice, well-to-do family is in my place of work right now, 'cause they know them too and isn't this a coincidence?* So, when it turns out that those folks I've been yammering on about have more than a few things missing when they get home, all I have to say is, "Well, goddamn if I wasn't just washing the dishes and minding my own business." In other words: "Oh, I'm not doing nothing over here, I don't know shit about fuck."

It's a great entry-level spying tactic. Play dumb.

The second way of spying will be painfully familiar to any woman who reads this. I don't know how to make it sound catchy, so I'll just say what it is: pretending to like or want something that you actually don't. In fact, you might think that thing is actually fuckin' disgusting, but you pretend that you want it as a distraction to get the other thing that you really want.

I'll give you an example. What Marty might call a hypothetical. Let's say that you've been tasked with spying on the owner of the only strip club in town or some such establishment. Then let's say that 'cause you're a girl, the only way you can think of to get in the door is to pretend like you want to be a stripper. You know how you do that? You actually apply to be a stripper, even though the idea of a bald redneck motherfucker staring at you from the tits down makes you homicidal.

So you're pretending like you want the job, like you'll just go broke and die if you don't level up to the lofty position of stripper in chief; you even hike your pants up your damn crack so he can see the outline of your ass, you're pretending you want this job so hard. Then it happens. Goddamn fucker asks you for a blow job. And looking at that cue ball turns your stomach so you never wanna even THINK about dick again, let alone suck one, and all you can think about is maybe trying to break that thing off to spare the other girls.

But instead of doing any of that, you smile, tilt your head to the side, and make like you're gonna go ahead and do what the man asks for. Well, you pretend (for the record, there was no way in hell I was gonna even look at Bobby Dean's pecker, let alone touch it). Thankfully, I was able to stop the train rolling down the tracks just in time to get the information I needed, sock the motherfucker in the balls, and run away fast.

This second type of spying is hard but rewarding. It's often the most effective, 'cause people are used to asking girls for shit that they don't want to give, and we're used to pretending like we wanna give it. Guaranteed you've had a waitress smile at you when she felt like spitting in your food, or a girlfriend who wanted to go home and get some sleep, but she stayed up letting you feel her up. I guess I'd say this tactic is for the ladies—not exclusively, but I think you get it. Hell, it's a safe bet that almost every woman you've ever met feels like she's part spy. Bond should have been a woman, or at least those Bond girls should have led him to his death by now.

The last type of spying, the one that I find the most cowardly and predictable, and which should only be used as a last resort, is the kind that employs the use of wiretaps, down-and-out criminals who are facing long sentences, and video-recording devices. That shit doesn't require the skill and patience and bravery of the first two kinds of spying. Sure, I bet FBI fuckers would disagree, but how come I've managed to stay out of cuffs for the past few years with only my wits and my dwindling network of relations, and they haven't nailed Marty Byrde even though they've got money, tech, and manpower? It's because they're snitching cowards who think they know goddamn everything, so someone like me can get past them real easy.

See, it's all always gonna loop back to that, to knowing that you might not know anything. People have been telling me that I'm a know-nothing piece of shit since I could walk, so I don't assume that I got things figured out, which is why I'm always working myself up trying to figure shit out. But those fuckin' government zombies? They think they know all the different categories of people that exist: the criminal, the wife, the drug lord, the money launderer, the kingpin, the dirtbag strip club owner, the Langmores even. Even if they put the Langmores in their own category (which they wouldn't because who the FUCK gives a shit about the Langmores), they wouldn't get it right.

When you spy on someone, when you truly spy on them, you're admitting that there's parts of them you don't know. Like when Marty spied on his own wife. He was saying to himself: "There's something I don't know about the woman I married, something that got by me, and I have to find out." Now, I'm not saying I think it's a good idea to spy on your wife in general—that would be a whole other book, and I don't think I'm a marriage expert, to tell you the truth. I don't have the interest. I'm just saying that he had good instincts to know that something wasn't right.

Spying isn't for people with a weak nature. It's not for cowards (unless you're a fuckin' FBI snitch). It takes a lot of skill, patience, time, and sometimes a strong stomach, but ultimately it's worth it, not just 'cause of what you'll learn about other people, but because what you learn about people can be carried over into what you know about people you meet in the future. You learn about different patterns, habits, and values, and those can always be carried over to new situations, whether that's work or your personal life.

Hopefully, if you practice, you'll learn that you're the type of person who has the stomach for spying. Hopefully you learn that you're the type of person who can sit and wait. Hopefully you learn that you're the type of person who can admit when they need more information than what they've got—that is, that you're the type of person who's ready and willing to learn.

If you discover, however, that you're the type of person who doesn't have a spy's instincts, if you find out that you get sick thinking about really looking at people for who they are, then spying might not be for you. If you're the type of person who reads this and still thinks that under the right circumstances, you'd be willing to turn folks you know over to the law, then read no further, because you think you know yourself and the people around you. You think you have the power of moral judgment. Remember, it's the worst type of motherfuckers who think they know shit when they don't. And government snitches? They're the worst offenders by far.

This is what my daddy would have called a real turning-point type of moment. If you're willing to spy on everybody and collect their sins, you gotta be willing to get taken down yourself. No exceptions.

CHAPTER

8

FIND YOUR IDOLS

The first time I heard any kind of hip-hop, it was Tupac, and it was an accident. Russ and Boyd thought it would be a good scam for me to hang out with some lake tourists one summer, see if I could steal their wallets with their parents' credit cards, whatever cash they happened to have. Boyd even thought if I could get one of them boys to knock me up, then we'd eventually get them to send us money for the baby. I didn't think they were serious about that one, but I told them to go fuck themselves anyway. The idea that they would even mention that shit was disgusting.

I was nervous getting face-to-face with tourists. I was used to stealing from them behind their backs, so it was weird getting to know them first. Not 'cause I had any moral hang-ups about it, but because even though those kids were the same age as me, it was like we were a different fuckin' species. I mean, these people were completely open to me, let me know how much money they had to spend and where they got it—didn't even occur to them to protect themselves from me. To me, it was like they were lambs tryin' to share beers with a lion. I was being raised to be a dangerous animal and those kids were housebroken is what I'm saying.

Thing is, with most of the kids I would see summer after summer, they didn't notice me one way or the other, even if we were hanging out, so it wasn't even a big deal to try and steal from them or nothing. Takin' candy from a baby.

I thought it was exciting at first. At first. Then it got boring real fucking fast. Those kids thought I was their redneck chaperone; kept

71

asking me where to get pot and begging for my uncles to buy us beer. It was too easy. They'd ask for beer and we'd tell them it cost more than it did, which in my opinion is hardly stealing. It's more like a commission or something like that.

Anyway, it was shaping up to be a pretty easy summer except that I couldn't fuckin' STAND these kids. I spent the least amount of time with them that I could. One of them, this boy with a name I can't remember, he was going to go to the university of I don't give a FUCK or something, he had a brand-new Ford Explorer. Shiny and black. I don't know how he kept that thing so shiny with all the dust and the dirt roads, but I guess he must have been proud of that thing, 'cause it gleamed. He'd take me and his friends ridin' around nearly every other day with the air-conditioning blasting. I remember his girlfriend was always getting her hair caught in her lipstick because of the AC breeze. And she'd say, "I hate this fuckin' car." And in my head I'd say, *Me. Too.*

One day we're driving along and this fuck-nugget is talking about how his daddy wants him to be a lawyer but he wants to be an architect and how he and his girlfriend with the lipstick are making plans and how sad they'll be when they go to school and they're apart. Just when this is all makin' me too sick to handle, this song comes on: "Me Against the World." All the dipshits started jumping around and I didn't even know who the fuck it was until someone yelled out the name: Tupac. The song got me, like it was saving me from these crazy-ass rich people.

All I could hear was the song, all I could hear was Tupac talking about the bad shit he'd seen and was going through, and the crazy shit he had to do to get by, and it fucked me up, but in a good way. I carved out a little piece of property in my mind that belonged to me and me alone when that song came on. I know that there are a lot of stupid-ass kids who think that they can relate to that song. I know it. But when he's talking about nobody caring about whether he's alive or dead, I felt that in my body. I stole that kid's iPod later that night. Thankfully this kid had all kinds of rap downloaded, and I was hooked on it. Especially Biggie.

I'll always have a soft spot for Tupac because he was my first, but Biggie is the real deal to me. He came out of some hard-ass shit when he

was coming up as a rapper, and he turned that shit into gold. Ever listen to the song "Gimme the Loot"? I know it's not one of his big hits but I highly recommend it—what you hear is someone who's actually been through the thing that he's going on about. Stickups. On both ends. Like you can hear that he'd had shit taken from him and he'd taken shit from other people. It's not just a bunch of lip service. It's a big deal to me that someone would talk out in the open about being pushed into crime. But then the B.I.G. could also turn around and deliver something smooth and fun like "Juicy." He really showed me that human beings have range.

Did you know that just before signing to his first major label, Biggie spent nine months in prison? I light a candle for Biggie every time I'm trying to level up and better myself.

Now, you may be asking yourself, "What should I do if I don't like rap?" I mean, I think it's a pretty serious mental condition to not like old-school hip-hop, but the point is: Loving someone gets you riled up. Find someone who you think is a badass and hold them up high, look to them when you think you need help. Everybody needs something or someone to pray to, and for me, that's the Notorious B.I.G.

Russ and Boyd didn't think rap was real music, but they never even gave it a chance. Anyway, I think maybe I was glad to have Biggie, Tupac, Snoop, Nas, and a whole host of other icons all to myself—it was like having a secret potion that gave me a superpower to get through the day. There was something so personal about the way their songs made me feel. Like they were talking directly to me. Finding people you admire is an important part of not knowing shit about fuck sometimes. When I'm down and I don't know what I'm doing with my life, I don't have to know—I can just put my headphones on and turn the music up loud and disappear into their words. It helps me turn my brain off when I'm overthinking shit, because they've already done the thinking for me.

It's almost like Biggie and Tupac are the brothers I never had. Shit, it's like we have secrets. You know that Tupac song "Brenda's Got a Baby"? It's about a girl who gets pregnant by some sick fuck in her family and then she throws the baby away because she doesn't know what she's doing and no one ever gave her a fuckin' chance. I knew girls like that growing up. I had friends who I don't have anymore because of them getting knocked up by someone who didn't deserve to look at 'em, let alone touch them. But nobody ever talks about that shit. And when they do talk about it, it's a punch line. Makes me mad.

Tupac didn't think it was a punch line though. And sure, I wanted to go out and have fun, but I grew up surrounded by men who didn't know how to talk to women without getting them pregnant and I didn't want that for myself. No fuckin' way. So I just had my private relationship with my idols; didn't matter whether they were West Coast or East Coast, that shit doesn't matter to a girl from the Ozarks—only coast we got is the fuckin' lake.

Another reason to find someone to worship the way that I worship Biggie or Tupac? It helps you find your people. Like when I met Tuck at the Blue Cat. Hell, I know he was probably lying about liking rap, but I knew he was cool because he at least tried to lie to me about it.

So, it ain't necessarily about finding Biggie or whoever as your personal savior, but maybe more about finding your own personal icon, someone who you can relate to easily, someone who has had their share of drama and success. It doesn't even matter if they're alive or dead, just as long as their love helps you get through the goddamn day. The reason I hold Biggie and Tupac up as shining examples of what can get you to the next level is that they know how to turn a shit situation into gold. They came from a place where there was a lot stacked against them and they rose above it to great success. I know that they met a bad end, but their music still does it for people all over the world. I'm sure they never even thought about their music reaching a place like Osage Beach; thankfully for me, it did.

CHAPTER

9

ON LOVE

There's only two kinds of love you can have out here in the middle of nowhere. First, there's the kind of love you can get from someone who doesn't know how to fuckin' love you, who's going to hurt you, leave you, or make you wish they had left. These types usually end up in jail or dead or on drugs, and they're a hard pass for me. The second type of love you can seek out in the Ozarks is the love of Christ. I don't think I need to tell you why that doesn't appeal to me. I don't want nobody washing my sins away.

The sad truth is, both kinds of love usually end with kids. The first kind makes pretty damn sure you're going to get yourself pregnant and get left with the kid, and motherhood was never something that was in the cards for me. No fuckin' way. When you're a single mother, people expect you to be nurturing and kind, and, well, that just ain't who I am.

I once had a friend named Nikki; she got pregnant when we were about thirteen and she said about the stupidest thing I've ever heard any living human say. She said that she was going to have the baby because at least she'd have someone to love. You've gotta be kidding me.

Now, I know you probably think I'm a cold bitch for not understanding the desire for love when you're lonely, but I just so happen to think that if you're gonna have a kid, it's not their job to make you feel less alone. That's a lot of fuckin' pressure to put on a kid. And if I'm honest, I'm not convinced that Nikki loved that kid as much as she thought she was going to anyway. Her mom was a chain-smoking dope fiend, the baby daddy was long gone, and she had no recourse but to leave that screaming infant with her neighbor while she was at work. No sir, that shit ain't for me.

And besides, courtship has always felt so fuckin' sticky to me—I just never was sure how I feel about romance. And I'm not saying that to be cool or whatever, I just wasn't sure about it. In my mind, the best-case scenario was: Some redneck shitkicker president of the fuckin' 4-H club comes to your house with flowers and declares his intentions and soon enough your kid is the manager of a Walmart. So what.

Before I met Ben, I think I'd had one romantic night in my entire life, and the whole thing made me sick to my stomach. Some boy from town showed up on my doorstep like a lost puppy, and I'll be goddamned if he didn't have flowers and candy for me. Russ and Boyd would have split his lip and his tight jeans if they hadn't been out drinking.

Anyway, that boy had a cute face and a sunshine earnest smile but he didn't have much else going for him. I remember thinking, *You should be grateful that someone likes you, Ruth.* But I mainly wanted to punch that smile off his face.

We rode around in his truck and went to the lake and drank as much Boone's Farm as we could without getting sick. Then he asked me if I wanted to meet his dogs. That's where shit went sideways, 'cause I love a sweet dog. So we took the drive to his place even though we were both pretty wavy by then. Once we get there, I see a dog that's about the size of a motorcycle that looks like it's half wolf or some shit, and it starts charging at me and knocks me on my back. But that dog was just sayin' hi, and then I thought, *This guy ain't so bad. He's got a cool dog.* But then he did something that turns my stomach to think about to this day. I was petting the dog, running my fingers through its fur, thinking about how I wished it were my dog, and then this little redneck motherfucker tried to tangle his fingers up with mine while I'm petting the dog.

Now, at first fuckin' blush this may not seem like much to you, but it was disgusting. He was *using* the dog to touch me.

I asked him to take me home but he wouldn't budge. He just kept trying to touch my hands and my knees on the sly, acting like he was just petting his dog. I can't even think of that dog now without getting a little sick. And don't get me wrong, I don't mind if a guy tries to touch you, if a guy wants to be direct, because then you can directly reject him, but this I-didn't-mean-to-touch-you-but-I'm-touching-you bullshit? No thank you.

That's why I liked Ben. Well, there were a lot of reasons I liked Ben, but what got me in the first place was that he was direct. He was

the first person who I could tell was actually looking at me, like really looking at me. Every other person I ever talked to in my life, they didn't look. And hey, there's a big part of me that doesn't want to be stared at, like not at all, but there's something particular about having someone really look at you and like what they see.

I don't get a lot of softness in my life. When folks seem like they want to warm up to me, I can't help but think what they may want. Sure, there's the softness I feel toward Wyatt and Three, but that's different. That's protective love, that's love of family. What I'm talking about is something I never felt before, toward anyone. Ben was persistent and smart and good-looking. Another thing that got to me was the way he wanted to figure out what I like. He wanted to figure out how to make my life better. First time I've really felt like someone wanted to take care of me. And hell, he was a good time too. When he wanted to be.

Truth is, I've never been loved by anyone except Ben. I don't know if I'll ever have that again. He showed up in my life just when I needed someone on my side, but then he disappeared just as fast. It's scary losing something that you don't think you'll ever get back. I didn't know that feeling before. Sure, the Byrdes said they fuckin' loved me, but they meant it the way that some people say they love something that services their lives; I could have been a car wash that does good work, a two-for-one meal, a good tailor, a babysitter. I was loved as a utility, not as a person. Ben loved me as a person. His happiness was tied up in my happiness. His life was tangled up with mine because he had no choice once he met me.

You know what really made me fuckin' sad about Ben though? He spent so much of his life having these attacks of delusion and paranoia, times where he thought people were out to get him, when he thought that there were conspiracies and shit like that, and this last time *he was right*. He was right that there was a darkness behind everything around him. That there were liars. And conspiracies. And evil. That's what breaks my fuckin' heart every time I think about him. Sure, he was hurting, but he wasn't wrong. He wasn't wrong.

And that's how he got himself killed: The delusion became the real thing.

Now, look—I don't know shit about love except this: Love means exposing your belly to a knife. It's all risk, and even though I've lived a life full of risk, this isn't the kind that I have a lot experience in. I'm sure there are some people in this world who are set up to love, but I'm not one of them, that's for goddamn sure. If you're gonna love, you need to be able to recover from it, because it will gut you. And I know people say it's worth it, but I wholeheartedly disagree. It's dangerous. I'm an open fuckin' wound and I don't know when that'll change.

Unless you got a lot of love around you, unless you were brought up to love, unless you were trained to do it and see it and recognize it, then I recommend you stay the fuck away from it.

CHAPTER

10

NO ONE IS YOUR DADDY

No one is going to protect you or guide you or love you the way that you *think* a father should. That thing doesn't exist. No one out there in the world is observing you and waiting for the exact moment when you need help. No one wants to help. If they do help you out sometime, it's a fuckin' accident of fate. They just happened to be there when you needed it—wrong place, wrong time. Chivalry ain't nothing more than a calculation to get a want, a desire. Every time Marty Byrde offered me anything, it was because it helped him. Not because it helped me. Even when it just so happened to help me.

Your dad isn't your daddy. Most dads aren't daddies. No one can fuckin' live up to your standard, so let it go. I'm not saying that all dads are Cade Langmores, but even guys like Marty Byrde make shit dads. It doesn't matter if it's some middle-class asshole or the fuckin' CEO of Apple, most dads are shit, and if they're not shit, just remember this: They won't be with you forever. Even if you think you have father of the year, you're gonna have to move on with your goddamn life and grow up someday. Hopefully.

I once read a book when I was a kid about a dad who would read books to his daughter at night and they would go on these fuckin' magical adventures together while they read, and I was like, "Is this science fiction, 'cause it doesn't exist."

Not on this planet.

Your boyfriend isn't your daddy. I hope that's fuckin' obvious, but I can clarify. Your boyfriend might seem like a good substitute for a father type, but he isn't. You know why? 'Cause he's fuckin' you and that shit ain't right. Don't get that mixed up with wanting a daddy. No one is here to take care of you. If they just so happen to meet your needs in the moment, it's because they're meeting *their* needs. If you like the way your boyfriend fucks you, he's meeting your needs 'cause that's what he wants for himself. If he buys you dinner, it's 'cause he wants to think of himself as the type of asshole who goes around paying for shit, and plus, he's gotta eat too. It's all just an illusion.

Your employer is not your daddy. I cannot emphasize this one enough. Your employer is not your daddy. He or she does not owe you shit except your wages, and even then they might debate you.

I made the mistake of thinking of Marty like a mentor. Thinking of someone like a mentor is a hell of a mistake, because guess what a mentor is almost exactly like? A daddy. Once I started thinking of Marty like he was my mentor, I started trying to earn his approval; once I started to earn his approval, I started to think that he fuckin' owed me his approval. Again, your employer doesn't owe you shit except your wages.

I know that this one is a hard one to catch, 'cause you go lookin' for a daddy without even meaning to. You feel a hollow place where love and acceptance and all that shit should be and you wanna fill it. Now, I've been pretty smart considering where I come from, and I didn't go around fuckin' everybody I met or doing a shit ton of drugs or drinking myself silly, so I'll give myself that. I did, however, go around looking for people's good opinion. Oh, it may not seem like that at first 'cause of how I talk, but I want it just like everybody else—and that's the hard truth.

There was that one night that Marty and Wendy took me into their home all protective-like because of my dad going psycho on Charlotte, and for a second I thought I was maybe making inroads to patching together something like a family.

When I was at their house, the Byrdes acted like caring for each other was no big deal, and it was like being blinded by something bright. It was fuckin' strange, but then it was beautiful and then I wanted it. I wanted to be surrounded by people who would kill for me and then make me pancakes.

See, the myth of my family was that we'd kill for each other, but after havin' the Langmore men raise a hand to me enough times, I had to take them at their actions instead of their words. If it wasn't Russ or Boyd popping me in the face like a misbehaving dog, it was my father smackin' me around for not being the right person at the right time, and if it wasn't him then it was Marty letting the cartel unleash hellish violence on me.

I've never gotten a break in my life.

Searching for the perfect father has always led me to shameful action. The way I let Cade hold power over me for such a long time even though he was such a shit dad makes me feel sick when I think about it. But then I also feel ashamed when I think of how fast I started wanting to please the Byrdes, how protective I became in such a short time. I mean, hell, I pointed a gun at my own father to save Charlotte from getting dragged all over the Ozarks while Daddy looked for that cartel money.

Money.

Now that's one thing that might be your daddy. Money can feed you, can house you, can support you. Money helps you take care of yourself. If you're in search of a missing goddamn parent, maybe money is where to look.

CHAPTER

11

TRY THINGS FIRST

None of the men in my family are going to win father of the year, even if the nominating field was narrowed down to trailer parks, but they did teach me that practice makes perfect. You gotta check shit out before you make a move. You have to circle around what you want so you know what to do when you're near enough to get it. And I'll be damned if Cade, Russ, and Boyd didn't always ask me to plan ahead when goin' in for something we wanted. Whether the task at hand was getting our hands on an expensive boat part or takin' money from a hotel room, I was always encouraged to observe things in detail before making a fuckin' move.

That doesn't mean that Cade and them didn't do stupid shit on impulse. Of course they did. All three of them would have their fuckin' lives to show for it if they had complete control over every stupid thought they had. But at their best? Those assholes knew how to navigate all kinds of situations. Hard thing is, now that I put it together, seems like they had a knack for planning when things were rough, but didn't know how to do shit when things were good. Just when I was starting to make money was when they started behaving at their worst.

Some people just don't know what to do with good luck, and good luck just don't stick to some people. That's a fuckin' lesson for ya.

When I was a kid, I remember wanting a bike real bad, but when Cade finally got around to getting one for me (don't ask me how, but you can assume and I won't be offended), he didn't know how to teach someone to ride a bike—he couldn't ride one himself. He just told me to suck it up and get on. I had to learn the hard way, or maybe that's just the Langmore way. Had to get back on a half dozen times before I could make that thing go, but I remember through all the pain and Cade yelling at me about learning something he didn't even know how to teach me to do, I suddenly got it in my mind that I had to learn. It wouldn't have been worth all the scraping and the hurt if I didn't learn how to do this thing. So even though Daddy was being an asshole, making me get back up when he didn't know shit, I was able to push through. That's the important thing. Trying things is how you know if it's worth the injury.

I lost a good chunk of my pride and my skin on that particular day, but I learned something when Cade looked at me, all scuffed up and bloody, and said, "Well, now we know you don't like bikes, baby girl." You can only find out if you like something by doing it once. Sure, there might be exceptions. Like, I know I don't want to eat raw chicken, ever. I don't. I'm not going to, and there'd have to be a hell of a lot of money in it for me if I did. Most other things though? You gotta try them.

Have you ever been to a "world-famous" type of place where they say they have the best fried chicken or barbecue or key lime pie, but when you ask someone who works there if the key lime pie is really such a big deal, they look at you and say they don't know, 'cause they're a vegan and they haven't fuckin' tried it? That type of situation is exactly the type of situation you never wanna be in: working at a place where you don't know what anything tastes like 'cause you've got a hard-on for chickens and cows, so you're just assuming that the shit you serve is delicious and you've never even tried it.

No, you gotta try things first. It's exciting to try new things, to learn new skills. You think I would have guessed that I would be good at laundering money? Fuck no. Absolutely not. It was just an instinct that it would do me some good. I tried it, and you know what? I'm good at it. I am good at it. I surprised myself, and that's another point: You're gonna surprise yourself when you try new things.

When I was a kid, wanting that bike, thinking Cade hung the moon before he went off to prison, I never would have thought I'd not only take charge of a casino but would leave it behind too. I never thought

I'd be the kind of person who could just leave things behind. The type of person who wears a suit to work. The type of person who has options. I guess what I'm talking about is imagination, in a way. There's really two parts to it: You gotta imagine yourself in new situations, and you gotta put yourself in new situations.

Sometimes trying things first means "fuck yeah let's jump out of a plane" and then sometimes it means "let's learn how to properly jump out of a plane." It's both things, and those things sometimes bump up against each other. Sometimes you let yourself down when you're trying something out. I know I've let myself down plenty. That's why you gotta create room for mistakes. I'm never going to be the person who can keep things all the way under control all the time. So it's important to know who the fuck you are when you go into new situations.

My uncles were my first kill, and that's something that's gonna follow me around forever. When you do something you haven't done before, you take all your past experiences with you, which means I'll always do things like a killer. When you plan new things, you bring your experiences with you, which means I'll always plan like a killer. They go hand in hand. Even though it broke my fuckin' heart to hurt Wyatt again, I knew I had to try being honest with him about his dad, 'cause lying to him about it, letting him make up other stories about what had happened, that shit was driving him crazy. It wasn't honest to let him live like that, and being honest was a new thing to try. I didn't have a plan about what to say after that or what to do. But I knew I had to try it.

Sometimes you fail. Sometimes you try something new and you fuckin' hate it. Or you make a plan and it fails. Sometimes new experiences sit in your mouth like food gone bad. When you try things, be willing to accept what you might lose. It's called fuckin' bravery.

CHAPTER
12

DON'T EXPECT ANYONE TO
FEEL SORRY FOR YOU

If you are from a particularly rough background, it can be tempting to use your sob story to make people feel bad for you. I know, because from time to time I've done it—a few times without even meaning to. Now, this wasn't always my fault. There's a specific type of person who feeds off of other people's tears and trouble. This is the type of person who mentors underprivileged kids at school or volunteers at homeless shelters and spends time with people who've got less, not so they can necessarily do any good in the world, but so they can feel good about *themselves*. After years of experimenting, I'd say it's best to avoid this kind of person.

Part of the reason I know my way around this particular subset of people is because not having a mother makes people wanna bend over backward: It just breaks their hearts. Makes twisting people around your finger a little easier than it should be. When I used to tell folks how my mother died, they'd just about dig themselves a grave, it'd make them so sad. I could even see a flicker of pity in Helen's eyes when I told her about my mother. She's not your typical type of sympathy freak, but I knew that I had earned some kind of respect the minute she seen where I come from, what I had to pull myself out of.

Bootstrapping is what assholes call it. No matter who you are, folks love a story where someone is just rolling around in the muck and then they ascend to some kind of glory. They climb the mountain, they defeat the monster. In my case the mountain is poverty and the monsters are my family. But I got ghosts to fend off too: my mother and father, both my uncles, and, for a while, it was like Wyatt was a ghost too, just a living one. Life has been fuckin' painful for me in a lot of ways, but profiting off of it just ain't something I've been able to master. Problem is, once you get lost in telling people your troubles, you lose yourself too.

Thankfully I learned this lesson young. When I was little, like seven or eight, I had a friend at school with a real nice family, and nice families are hard to come by out here, believe me. Her name was Jennifer—she didn't even shorten it to Jenny, and I thought that was real fuckin' elegant. Anyway, I was fascinated by her and her family 'cause they owned their house and they ate meals together. It was a small house and the meals weren't gourmet or nothing, but they were a real family. She even had a sister, which I thought was an achievement or something because I had always wanted a sister. Her name was Melissa, which I learned was Greek for honeybee or some shit. They let me hang around their backyard and kitchen a few days a week after school, and I still remember those times feeling like the most comfortable I've ever been in my skin.

Jennifer's mom would do this really nice thing where she would have me pony up to the kitchen counter on a barstool while she made us a snack, and Jennifer would blurt out something like, "You know that Ruth don't have a mom?" And Jennifer's mother would say something like, "Well no, I didn't, but maybe let Ruth speak for herself."

She'd ask me about my mom and I'd make shit up because I didn't know much about her. You could say that my mom was the first thing I didn't know shit about. And I know now that Jennifer's mom probably knew I was full of shit, but because she felt sorry for me she let it slide. That was a big goddamn deal for me. You see, folks didn't want nothing to do with Cade Langmore's daughter. Kids would joke about me having lice, or say that I looked dirty, and parents sure as shit didn't want to deal with Cade, so I was kind of a loner even among the poorest kids. It was a shock to me that Jennifer's mother would take me into her home at all, let alone feed me cookies and milk while I fed her bullshit and lies about who I was.

One afternoon, Cade had started drinking kind of early even for Cade, meaning he was shit-faced by the time I had wandered home from

Jennifer's house. He had that stale smell like he'd been smoking and drinking in a closed room, letting his thoughts run around in a circle like he always did when he was alone and up to no good. He asked me where I been and I said Jennifer's. And he said, *Jennifer.*

I think it's a universal truth that kids can tell with one word or look from their parents whether they're about to be on the receiving end of a beatin', and I could tell here that for no good reason, Cade Langmore was ready to discipline me, maybe for attempting to make friends with a good girl. Maybe 'cause I said it like I expected him to understand why I'd be somewhere else. Both were unacceptable offenses to my daddy, and he lunged forward to grab me by the arm, but as I hadn't been drinking all afternoon in the gray light of a trailer, I was able to dart away from his tobacco-stained grasp.

There was no question in my mind where I'd go. I ran to Jennifer's house just as fast as I could. She didn't live far, but her neat little house felt like it was thousands of miles away from my tin can of a trailer. When I got there, I explained the situation to Jennifer's mom as best I could. Said I was scared of my daddy but didn't want to get him into trouble, asked if I could stay till he cooled off. Her mom looked at me with the sympathy of a saint, wrapped her arms around me, and said, "Stay for dinner." Which was the invitation I'd been angling for since I met them, to be honest.

We hadn't so much as started setting the table before there was a knock at the door—more of a pounding, really. And like he was speaking a language that only the two of us could understand, I knew that it was my daddy on the other side of that thin plank of wood. Jennifer's mom went to the door, acting like she didn't know who was there. When she opened it, Cade said, "Thank you for callin', miss."

I couldn't believe the level of betrayal. She called him. I told this woman I was afraid of getting my ass kicked, and she called my daddy to pick me up and finish the job. I thought I had her sympathy, but what I really earned that day was her fear. She didn't know I was from one of *those* families. It's not that she didn't feel nothing for my situation—I'm sure she did in a TV-movie-of-the-week kind of way—it's that she wouldn't do shit for me. She didn't keep me through dinner, she didn't call social services, she just called my daddy and removed herself from the situation altogether.

Funny thing is, Daddy was kind of soft on the way home. He was still all in the wash with drink, but he could see my pain about the situation. He said, "Ruthie, ain't no one ever gonna make your life better 'cause they feel sorry for ya. Ain't gonna happen. Sorry, baby girl, you're stuck with me. Less you wanna go to kid lockup."

That day I learned that pity is a bride's veil people wear to say to the world that they're pure from the sin of judgment.

The first time I sat down with Wendy, I'd just gotten a black eye from Russ. She fixed it up and I imagined for a second what it would be like if I were Wendy Byrde's daughter. What if I were Charlotte Byrde? Would I get pancakes every morning? Would we have deep conversations? Would my new mom have that moment where she realizes that I'm grown up and I can make my own decisions? Would I go to fuckin' college? All of that flooded into my brain while she was patting my cheek real soft with a cotton swab, and I felt that rotten Langmore luck running through my body, infecting me.

I did think that after everything Marty had seen me go through, he'd have a little empathy when Frank Jr. put me in the hospital. At that point I had fuckin' killed for Marty and his family; I'd been tortured for them too. So I thought that after having a front row to all of that hard luck, Marty would have a moment and say to himself, "I gotta kill Frank Jr. 'cause Ruth is like family." But he didn't. He was too scared. He was scared for his real family. Which is how I knew I put myself through too much shit for them. See, I always think of an angle, but I'd say I messed up when I thought they'd actually be able to see how hard things were from my point of view. But other people can't feel your bruises, can they?

With the Byrdes, I had started to believe that I had someone on my side. In part because of the hard work that I had done for them, but also because they had seen what I had to go through to get where I am. When Marty said I was untouchable, I really believed it. Fuckin' idiot that I am.

Never, ever expect someone to wave a magic wand and come through for you because they feel sorry for you and because they know you need it. That's the stuff that fuckin' fairy tales are made of.

CHAPTER

13

ALLOW YOUR MIND TO BE BLOWN

The two most mind-blowing events of my life were moments when I received compliments from men who were hard to please. I know that this doesn't sound like much, and it isn't, but I think it's important to look at it, to understand how a compliment can change your state of mind and open you up to new areas of development in your life.

First time I can remember getting a compliment in my life was from Daddy. We were workin' a house and he was showing me how I could get through a dog door 'cause I was so little. I don't remember the details of that job so well, being that I was so small, but I do remember him coaching me through it and being so goddamn pleased with the results. See, folks were already on high alert about my daddy, but they didn't know he'd have the brass balls to put his little girl to work. We waited until daylight when this family was at work and the kids at school and all of that. I slid through that doggy door, scrunching my shoulders up, reaching one limb at a time until I was through.

We were just doing a test run, but I remember that when I'd come out on the other side, I had decided to grab something from the bedroom just to prove that I'd gotten all the way into the house. I thought it was just a regular-ass watch, but it turns out it was a fuckin' Rolex. A stolen Rolex at that, 'cause the serial number had been scratched out. The owner couldn't exactly report a missing stolen Rolex, now could he? Daddy was so proud because he hadn't even asked me to do that, he was just seeing if he could take me on jobs, period, and when I came out with something of real value, I have to say he was fuckin' proud.

I hadn't seen that before. I didn't see it often.

After that, we went and pawned that watch. The guy at the pawn shop saw that the numbers were scratched and said he didn't take stolen shit. I got so upset I started crying, 'cause I thought I'd done something wrong. Cade just comforted me and asked the guy what he was upsetting his kid (me) for. I guess my tears embarrassed that fucker enough to make him buy the watch off of Daddy. That day, to my daddy, I was a genius, I was a cat burglar; he saw in me the same potential that I see to this day when I look at Wyatt, and that shit made me feel fuckin' amazing.

It was a mission of mine for a long time to get back to feeling like that with anyone in my family. Daddy was hard to please though; the targets always got bigger, so there was always a pretty good chance that I would fail. That first house going so smoothly might have been a fluke, or it might have been natural ability, but I guarantee that every time I fucked something up, Cade would look back to that first time and say it was "beginner's luck." So it's safe to say there wasn't any thought in my mind that I was going to make employee of the month with Marty Byrde.

I want to take a closer look at the moment I thought I was gonna kill Marty Byrde at the dock. At first, I was just in shock that Marty hadn't been electrocuted, but then something happened right after that, something that was just as extraordinary, this one little moment that changed my way of thinking. The moment just after Marty didn't die, he stepped onto the dock and turned to me and told me what a good job I was doing at the Lickety Splitz. He said it in this really sincere, down-to-his-penny-loafers kind of way. Like we were standing around a watercooler or some shit like that and not laundering money at a strip club in the middle of nowhere.

I don't know if I've made this clear, but I haven't exactly had a wealth of fuckin' praise in my life. Folks out here are hard on you, and a reputation is a nearly impossible thing to shake. I mean, at a certain point you say "fuck it" because if people are gonna treat you like a criminal, why would you put yourself through the paces of trying to prove them wrong? So this moment was a big deal. Since meeting the Byrdes, I'd been plotting and scheming to take their money, I had been focused on learning to launder, and I'd been trying to dodge catching hell from my daddy and my uncles for working for Byrde in the first place. It had never even dawned on me that I might be doing a good job.

Back on that dock with Marty, I think that was the first time since I was little that I'd thought about anything except pleasing my dad and my uncles and taking care of Wyatt and Three. I hadn't ever thought about what I want to do, let alone what I might be good at. That's why it's important to allow your mind to be blown. It's not always an explosion either—sometimes it's these little details like a casual com-

pliment or an observation someone makes about you that can change your course forever.

See, I think that that was the moment I started thinking a little bit about my future, about what I could provide for my family. Hell, I think it was the first time I started thinking about what I wanted besides survival. And it's not all about getting compliments either—it's more about letting your view of things change. From that first job with my daddy, I had just been trying to get by and not get caught and make things right with him because I thought that breaking and entering was my calling. To be fair, I was fuckin' great at it. I never thought I'd be good at something else, and I sure as shit didn't think I'd be good for someone else.

That was the first time that someone outside the Langmore clan had told me that what I was doing was good. At least it was the first time I could remember it. And with Marty came other folks who thought I was good at my job too. There were Wendy and Helen, there were the Byrde children who looked at me like I was a fuckin' person, there was a whole life that opened up to me with that one comment. If I hadn't had my eyes open to it, I might have missed it altogether. I might not have learned that I was actually good for something besides keeping the criminal baseline going at the trailer parks with my uncles and cousins. I guess I'm saying it was the first time I actually thought I had value.

Now, having your mind blown goes both ways. For instance, when I was a kid, I thought my daddy could get away with anything in the world, like he was Superman. Criminal charges just didn't quite stick to him like they did with other folks, and he could be charming with law enforcement, not unlike the way a rabid animal is deceptively cute before you reach out to touch it. Time after time I saw my daddy evade law enforcement, jail time, and probation violations. It wasn't until he killed my granddaddy that I saw the law come down on him. It was the most surprising thing I'd ever seen: Cade Langmore actually getting the sentence he had earned.

I wasn't surprised that he had done the thing, and I wasn't surprised that he got caught; I was surprised that he actually had to do the time. Up until that point he just seemed like someone who couldn't be caged.

But then he was. That's when I learned that everyone is a fuckup some-times. Anyone can get thrown in jail or killed or robbed or any manner of bad shit. My daddy was no exception and neither was I. That's an important one to remember. You gotta let the bad stuff blow your mind too because it teaches you. Since I started working for Marty, I've always held it in my mind that maybe he could fuck something up that he knows real well too. Maybe he'll forget to count someday.

I guess what I'm saying is that you don't want to get too used to one way of thinking about yourself or other people. I'm not what you would call an optimist, not by a mile, but if you allow your mind to be blown every once in a while, you might find out that you're actually pretty good at something.

People are surprising, trust me—sometimes for the better and some-times for worse. But if you're not looking, if you're not open to it, you're never going to get your mind blown.

CHAPTER
14

NO ONE IS YOUR MOMMY

It's hard to think of yourself as an orphan when you've got such a locally notorious family, but I guess that's what I am. In some way, that's what I've always been. Cade Langmore wasn't much into parenting except when he realized that kids were as good of a beer delivery service as anything. I remember wanting him to bring a decent woman home so bad. That is, until he brought someone home and I realized he didn't know his ass from his elbow when it came to women.

Her name was Gracie, or that's the name she went by at the club. She giggled a lot; she reminded me of a Coke that got shook too many times, the way you have to open it in small spurts so the carbonation won't fizz out. That's how Gracie was with laughing all the time. Anything you said was hilarious. Now, at the time, I thought this was stupid, but I couldn't help but like her 'cause she was kind in a way. Daddy perched this lady on his knee and slurred about how Gracie was his new friend.

She let me take her by the hand and show her into the trailer when she needed to use the bathroom. Her hands were soft and she had a fresh French-tip manicure. On the way into the bathroom she stopped, looked at the floor by the couch, and pointed to one of my worn-out dolls.

What's her name?

I'd be lying if I said that I didn't think this lady was nuts. She almost acted like she thought the doll was really alive.

I told her the doll's name was Rosie.

She drifted over to the doll on the floor and began to smooth her hair. I didn't know shit about how to do hair. She offered to show me how to braid it; she put my hands over hers and showed me how to fold one strand over the other over the other over the other until we had a braid. After we finished with that she went over to the bathroom and peed with the door open. Now, I'd seen Cade, Russ, and Boyd piss with their backs to me in the woods, but I'd never seen another female pee, so I got real embarrassed real fast. She laughed like that shook-up Coke again and closed the door.

Wasn't long after that Cade came in and knocked on the door, opened it, and found poor Gracie asleep on the toilet. While he helped her, he told me to get out and go bunk with my cousins. Last I saw of Gracie, she had her arm slung around Daddy's neck and was breathing something into his ear that didn't sound fizzy like her laughter. I think that was the closest I ever came to having a stepmom. Lasted about twenty minutes.

The next morning, I asked Cade when Gracie was gonna come back and he looked down at me like he was preppin' for a fierce-ass beatin'. I'm sure he was, but all that tension got broke by the howling sound of Russ's laughter. He said:

That little stripper whore ain't comin' back here after your daddy didn't pay his bill.

Before he could say anything else, Daddy was on him, tackling him, calling Uncle Russ all kinds of names before going silent while he worked on his face. I felt sick, 'cause even though I knew she wasn't much of a thinker, I still wanted her to come back.

People laugh at that book about the fuckin' bird lookin' for its mama, but that was me. Whether it was my friend Jennifer's mom, the occasional babysitter, or some tired stripper my dad brought home, I kept hoping that I'd find a woman I could look up to. I'd have even settled for an aunt. None of the men in my family ever did bring home another woman. That's for fuckin' sure. Russ didn't for obvious reasons, Boyd was shit with women, and Daddy was in lockup for most of my life. I never had the chance to get that stepmom or that cool aunt that I was always hoping for. I think that's what made it hard when I finally met women I could look up to. Didn't know how to interact with them.

It was one thing when Marty took me on to help him at the club and learn to launder. He was mainly keeping me from making trouble. Sure, I think he had some amount of kindness for me in his heart, but anytime I'm dealing with a man, I just remind myself that he's a man, you know? Not like he's gonna do nothing creepy, just like there's not a lot of heart and sensitivity there or something. But Wendy? She was completely different from any woman I'd ever met.

First, that lady is smart; she can talk her way out of any situation. When she's in a bind, it's almost like she gets more calm while she's also getting more angry at the same time. So she knows how to weave a trap for her enemies with her words. When I was a kid and I'd fantasize about who my mom was, I always thought she'd be the smartest person I ever met. Smarter than Russ and Boyd wouldn't be hard, but smarter than Cade would be something. I imagined that my mom would be the type of person who would tell me how good and smart I am after Cade had just told me how stupid and worthless I am.

Of course, Wendy's way with words turned vicious after everything with Ben. I've had Cade tell me I'm worthless, but I've never had someone go as far as she did when she said my loving Ben is what killed him.

That's the other thing about Wendy: She's a little scary. She scared the shit out of Wyatt when she thought he was threatening her daughter. That's something you gotta have respect for, and again, it's exactly the type of thing that I had my mom do for me a hundred times over in my head. I guess I always pictured a mother as being someone who is the ultimate defender. But here's the thing—mothers are defenders, but only for their kids. No one else. Wendy would kill for Charlotte and Jonah, but no one else, not even Marty. Not even her own fuckin' brother. Even Cade Langmore wouldn't have put out a hit on his own brother. Most despicable shit I've ever seen.

Watching her go toe-to-toe with Helen Pierce over their kids getting into trouble was just as terrifying as anything I'd seen my uncles pull during a fight, except it was with their words and emotions. That's some witchy shit the way mothers make each other feel bad. I never had seen it before.

Helen Pierce was definitely interesting as a mother type. She was so tough with her clients, so steely cool with Marty and Wendy, so unruffled even when she was pissed like a bull. But when it came to that kid of hers, holy shit, it was a totally different Helen. She'd murder anyone who came near her daughter, but she was also so tightly wrapped around her kid's finger that she didn't know which way was up. Watching those two talk to each other was fuckin' crazy. The little brat would scold her mother. If I had ever given that kind of lip to Cade Langmore, I'd still be in the hospital.

It's gonna sound kinda weird, but the most successful of the "mothering" types in my life is Darlene Snell. Now, before you go all cross-eyed about how fuckin' crazy Darlene Snell is, let me tell you one thing: She kills for the people she loves.

She's the only one who stuck up for me when I was all beat up in the hospital, and she thought it was important for Wyatt to make me a part of his life again. Yeah, she's a crazy-ass bitch who made my life harder in some ways, but as it happens, she's also someone I've come to admire. People thought they could write her off 'cause she was a hillbilly or get rid of her because she was fuckin' nuts, but she decided to be a thorn in the side of anyone in her way. That's a strength that I haven't seen in any of my dealings with the Byrdes, the KC mob, or Helen. She doesn't bend for shit. And she doesn't try to contradict what people think of her either. She's like the master of not knowing shit about fuck. If being the master of not knowing shit about fuck didn't totally contradict the whole fuckin' idea.

Even though Darlene surprised the hell out of me by coming through for me the way she did, she's still not family. Period. Sorry, it's like I said: *No one is your mommy.* Darlene could do nice things for me till her dying day and nothing else, but I still wouldn't call her Mother, 'cause if they don't consider you their kid, guess what? You're fuckin' not.

That woman killed her own husband, and I don't doubt for a minute that if I disappointed her she'd just chop my head off for fun. I got respect for her, but respect has limits, and you gotta be careful when you have a mother-shaped hole in your gut. I'm not saying I won't work with her—hell, I'm not even gonna say that I won't be friends with her—but it doesn't matter what anyone says about you being "like family" or "like a daughter"; saying "like" just means that you aren't. If you're really like someone's kid, the person in question just fuckin' points at you and says, "Hey, lay the fuck off, that's my kid." And then that's the last of it.

Folks don't need explanation for family, no matter what the size or shape of it, and except for Wyatt and Three, I'm not in one.

So, as much as you may want someone to fill in the gaps for you and be like a mother, they aren't. They can't be. You'll be so disappointed if you go there with them, trust me. I'm not saying don't take the good parts of someone who's offering you good things—I'm just saying they aren't really family.

CHAPTER

15

NOBODY KNOWS SHIT ABOUT FUCK—CONGRATULATIONS

I knew a guy who was trying to quit smoking and so he read a book about how to quit smoking; he got all pumped about it and started to picture his life without cigarettes and all of that. Then a few hours after he finished reading the goddamn book he went out and bought a pack of cigarettes and he still smokes to this day. This isn't that. I'm not trying to get you to win friends and influence people or quit smoking or organize your closet or any of that shit. I'm just telling you about what I've learned along the way, and this way of looking at the world has been key.

You know when you get to the end of some epic movie where the hero is supposed to do some big-shit thing, and then it turns out that the solution to their problem was there all the time? I guess you could say this is that ending:

You never knew shit about fuck.

Congratulations.

Now, it'll probably be an ongoing battle to admit to yourself on a daily basis that you *don't* know what you *think* you know and that there are things out there that you just *don't know at all*, but if you commit to not knowing, you can really learn a lot, because, well, you have everything to learn.

Situations might arise in the future where you'll say to yourself, "Well, I'm pretty sure I know what I'm doing here." But you gotta remember that that kind of thinking is the enemy. You can't assume you know shit, but I know it will be tempting. Even when you're doing your most average kind of daily tasks, you gotta keep yourself in check about how you approach those situations in which you think you know what you know. Remember, everything is suspect, everything is baby new. Whether that's your job, your best friend, your partner, or even your kids, wipe the slate clean every day. It'll pay off if you do.

I didn't know shit about the Byrde family when they got here, didn't know that they would be so complicated, didn't know that they'd end up being such a big part of my life. Honestly, I didn't figure that they'd end up knowing their shit. Same with everything else, there's what you see and what you get; those things are sometimes a lot further away from each other than you could know. I ended up being surprised with my jaw hangin' open so often you'd think I was trying to catch flies. Point is, people are surprising, life is surprising, and there ain't no one way to live it.

At this point in my life I've met useless people who were useful, smart people who were fuckin' dumb, and convicts who had more moral fiber than any churchgoing motherfucker I've ever met. If you'd have told me a couple of years ago that I'd end up bunked up with Darlene Snell and that my cousin Wyatt would be her lover, I would have laughed you out of town. But here I am, impressed with that crazy bitch. If you'd have told me that I'd be killing family because of how much I cared for a rich money-laundering family, I'd have thought you were fuckin' crazy. But here I am. Two dead uncles, a dead father, and no job to show for it. Not on that side of things anyway. I did get good at something though, which sounds like it goes against my beliefs, but trust me, it doesn't.

Getting good at something is different from knowing something. It's maybe the opposite. When you're getting good at something, you're allowing that there's always a way to do that something a little bit better than the way that you're doing it. Like an athlete. I think it's fine to try to get good at something, just so long as you don't get ahead of yourself trying to be the best. You'll never win like that. At least I won't. And I sure as shit haven't seen someone say they're the best and not get knocked the fuck off their pedestal.

A lot of what I'm talking about involves making mistakes, which sucks, because people fuckin' hate making mistakes. I know I do, 'cause when I make a mistake there's usually jail time, personal injury, or maybe even death on the other end of it.

Most of my life, I felt unlucky about what I'd been born into. I felt unlucky without a mother; I felt unlucky with Cade, and Russ and Boyd. The people around me made me feel like that luck would never get better, especially folks on the outside like teachers and counselors and others who were supposed to make me feel like hope was always an option. Nobody ever made me feel like hope was an option. When you grow up with people telling you that you would be fortunate if you managed to nab a full-time job at a Target twenty miles out of town, or to count yourself as having won the goddamn lottery if you manage to get a waitressing job at a Cracker Barrel off the highway, or that it'd be a fuckin' miracle if you stayed out a prison, you don't expect much from the future.

Sure, I wanted things for myself; I wanted things for Wyatt and Three. Everybody has fantasies about what they want—difference between a success and a failure is figuring out how to get there. The great thing about the rough way my life started out is that I didn't ever have it in my head that I deserved shit. Didn't think anyone owed me what I couldn't take. Whether that's money under the bed or a boat part I've been hunting down. I never had any intention of getting this far. I just always took the next step and the next. Not quite the same as stumbling around like you're blind drunk, but I think it's important that I didn't know what was gonna happen from one day to the next.

My whole life with the men in my family prepared me for that. I never got used to any kind of comforts—never had them, really. So how could I get ideas about what I should be? How could I get ideas about what I should have?

Truth is, nobody knows what they're doing. Including me. My advice is as good as anyone else's. All I can say is that every time I meet someone new, I know for a fact that they don't know shit; the only thing that's different person-to-person is how much they're willing to admit what they don't know. And after these past few years, I don't know if I'm actually any good at crime or if I'm a genius. I don't know if Ben was the love of my life or just some more fuckin' heartbreak. I don't know if Wyatt will ever truly forgive me, and I sure as shit don't know if I'll ever forgive myself.

Sometimes, I like to close my eyes and picture just a slightly different version of Cade, one who still robs a liquor store while he's on probation, but one who also knows how to smile at a mistake. In my mind, that version of Cade takes my face in his hands, like a dad in a movie or a TV show, and says, "Ruthie, baby girl, it's okay. Better luck next time."

I know what I've done, where I've been. I'm honest with myself. That's rare. If you can get to a point where you're honest with yourself, hats off to you, 'cause you've got the general population of the fuckin' world beat on that count.

Hopefully you found this helpful, and if you didn't find it helpful, maybe you found a strange kind of comfort in it. Wyatt and Three wouldn't say I'm the traditionally nurturing type, but I know that sometimes it's good to hear someone just give up the fuckin' game and say "I don't know." So one more time I'll say I don't know. I wish that when I was a kid, instead of having a bunch of men telling me the way it is, I had had just one person who could have looked at me and said, "Ruth Langmore, don't worry, nobody knows what they're goddamn doing. And that's a fact."

TITAN
BOOKS

144 Southwark Street
London SE1 0UP
www.titanbooks.com

Find us on Facebook: www.facebook.com/TitanBooks
Follow us on Twitter: @TitanBooks

Published by arrangement with Insight Editions, PO Box 3088, San Rafael, CA 94912, USA. www.insighteditions.com

A CIP catalogue record for this title is available from the British Library.

ISBN: 978-1-78909-968-3

Publisher: Raoul Goff
VP Licensing and Partnerships: Vanessa Lopez
VP Creative: Chrissy Kwasnik
VP Manufacturing: Alix Nicholaeff
Editorial Director: Katie Killebrew
Designer: Lola Villanueva
Editor: Matt Wise
Editorial Assistant: Sophia R Wright
Senior Production Manager: Greg Steffen
Senior Production Manager, Subsidiary Rights: Lina s Palma

A special thanks to Jed Rapp Goldstein, Julia Garner, Chris Mundy, and Jason Bateman.

ROOTS of PEACE   REPLANTED PAPER

Insight Editions, in association with Roots of Peace, will plant two trees for each tree used in the manufacturing of this book. Roots of Peace is an internationally renowned humanitarian organization dedicated to eradicating land mines worldwide and converting war-torn lands into productive farms and wildlife habitats. Roots of Peace will plant two million fruit and nut trees in Afghanistan and provide farmers there with the skills and support necessary for sustainable land use.

Manufactured in Turkey by Insight Editions

10 9 8 7 6 5 4 3 2 1